border to border · teen to teen · border to border · teen to teen · border to border

Teens in

Nigeria

by Pamela Dell

Content Adviser: Marida Hollos, Ph.D.,
Professor of Anthropology,
Brown University

Reading Adviser: Katie Van Sluys, Ph.D.,
Department of Teacher Education,
DePaul University

Compass Point Books ◆ Minneapolis, Minnesota

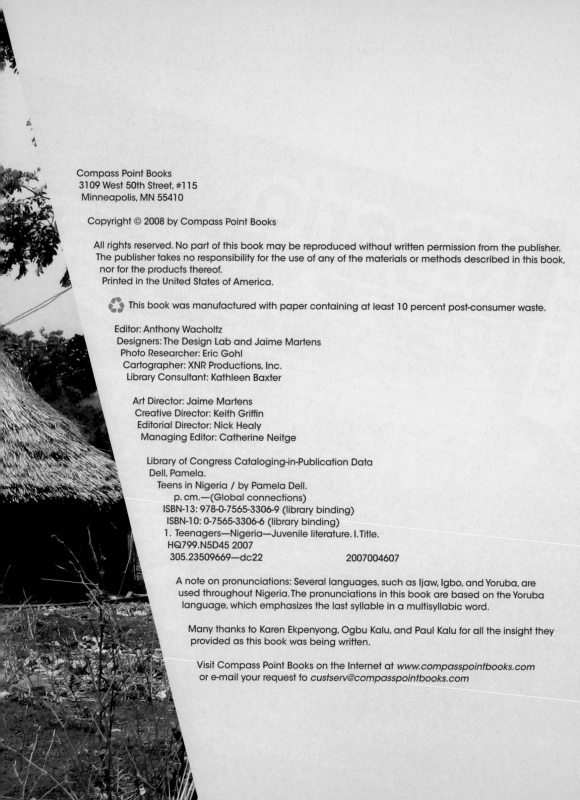

Compass Point Books
3109 West 50th Street, #115
Minneapolis, MN 55410

This book was manufactured with paper containing at least 10 percent post-consumer waste.

Editor: Anthony Wacholtz
Designers: The Design Lab and Jaime Martens
Photo Researcher: Eric Gohl
Cartographer: XNR Productions, Inc.
Library Consultant: Kathleen Baxter

Art Director: Jaime Martens
Creative Director: Keith Griffin
Editorial Director: Nick Healy
Managing Editor: Catherine Neitge

Library of Congress Cataloging-in-Publication Data
Dell, Pamela.
Teens in Nigeria / by Pamela Dell.
   p. cm.—(Global connections)
ISBN-13: 978-0-7565-3306-9 (library binding)
ISBN-10: 0-7565-3306-6 (library binding)
1. Teenagers—Nigeria—Juvenile literature. I. Title.
HQ799.N5D45 2007
305.23509669—dc22   2007004607

A note on pronunciations: Several languages, such as Ijaw, Igbo, and Yoruba, are
used throughout Nigeria. The pronunciations in this book are based on the Yoruba
language, which emphasizes the last syllable in a multisyllabic word.

Many thanks to Karen Ekpenyong, Ogbu Kalu, and Paul Kalu for all the insight they
provided as this book was being written.

Visit Compass Point Books on the Internet at *www.compasspointbooks.com*
or e-mail your request to *custserv@compasspointbooks.com*

Table of Contents

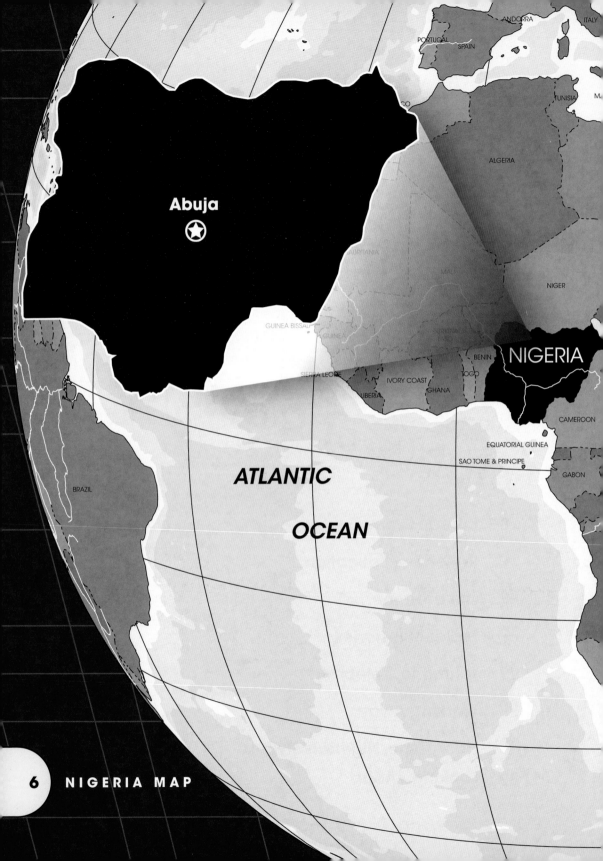

Abuja
★

NIGERIA

GUINEA BISSAU
GUINEA
SIERRA LEONE
LIBERIA
IVORY COAST
GHANA
TOGO
BENIN

BURKINA

MALI

MAURITANIA

ALGERIA

NIGER

ANDORRA
ITALY
PORTUGAL
SPAIN
TUNISIA

CAMEROON

EQUATORIAL GUINEA
SAO TOME & PRINCIPE
GABON

BRAZIL

ATLANTIC

OCEAN

BULGARIA

GEORGIA
AZERBAIJAN
ARMENIA

TURKMENISTAN

TAJIKISTAN

TURKEY

CYPRUS
LEBANON
ISRAEL
JORDAN

SYRIA

IRAQ

AFGHANISTAN

NEPAL

BHUTAN

IRAN

BANG

EGYPT

KUWAIT

QATAR
U. A. E
SAUDI ARABIA

OMAN

OMAN

PAKISTAN

INDIA

SUDAN

ERITREA

YEMEN

DJIBOUTI

SOMALIA

ETHIOPIA

ATIC REPUBLIC
IE CONGO

UGANDA

RWANDA
BURUNDI

KENYA

**INDIAN
OCEAN**

TANZANIA

ZAMBIA

MALAWI

MOZAMBIQUE

ZIMBABWE

BOTSWANA

SWAZILAND

LESOTHO

7

NIGERIANS ARE A DIVERSE PEOPLE—diverse in their ways of living, their religious beliefs, and their education. Most belong to Nigeria's three largest ethnic groups: the Igbo, the Yoruba, and the Hausa-Fulani. The rest are members of the nation's more than 250 smaller ethnic groups. Islam and Christianity are the major religions, but there are many followers of traditional Nigerian religions of all kinds.

While some of the teens are full-time students, others work all day long and never even see a classroom. Many live in one-room rural huts. Others live a modern lifestyle in the country's bustling urban centers. Today young Nigerians are waiting longer to marry, but many still wed at age 16 or younger. Nigeria's teenagers, a population that numbers in the millions, belong to a country still struggling to become a stable, well-managed democracy. Nigeria faces ethnic and religious conflict, economic collapse, poverty, and the AIDS epidemic, which are collectively taking a huge toll. Naija, as Nigeria is affectionately known by those within the country and those who have left their native land, is in some ways a boiling cauldron ready to bubble over. For Nigerian teens of the 21st century, the challenge is finding hope in a nation trying to emerge from its struggles.

Students in most Nigerian schools are required to wear uniforms.

1

In Need of Education

IN SEPTEMBER, A MONTH AWAY FROM THE END OF NIGERIA'S LONG RAINY SEASON, windswept streets and steady downpours do not stop millions of students from returning to school after a monthlong break. In each of the nation's 36 states and the Federal Capital Territory, classes are starting up for the year.

The Republic of Nigeria is Africa's most populated nation. But in a country where the vast majority of people have a low income, being able to go to school is not always easy. Young people are needed at home to help the family earn a living. Many have no means to get to school if the nearest one is not within easy walking distance.

Additionally, there are few free schools at any grade level, and money for tuition, supplies, uniforms, and various fees is hard to come by. But there are students who are determined to get an education in a system that has a long way to go to serve all of them properly.

Meeting students' needs for a decent education is a problem of extreme proportions. This includes providing up-to-date textbooks, well-trained teachers, and decent facilities.

The situation is made even more challenging by the fact that the student-age population is so great in Nigeria. More than half the nation's population is 19 years old or younger. Of Nigerians ages 5 through 17, nearly 81 percent attend school, though the classrooms may be severely ill-equipped. At the high school

Political Corruption

A series of corrupt and brutal military dictatorships in Nigeria have come and gone—usually by way of a violent *coup d'etat*, or revolution. The nation's vast resources have been mismanaged. Billions of dollars coming into Nigeria have been squandered, embezzled, or otherwise wasted by the series of political regimes that have held power. Leaders are often tempted to make off with funds meant for national education. Additionally, conflicts, disagreements, and even a civil war have divided people along ethnic and religious lines.

Speaking for the South East Youth Coalition (SEYC), a group of 35 youth associations in southeastern Nigeria, Chibuzor Ekwenye recently expressed the frustrations of an entire generation. "In us, the sum total of success or failure is reflected," he said, during a meeting with members of Nigeria's People's Democratic Party. "We bear the final brunt of government policy. When it affects our parents adversely, it reflects onto us and our well being. That is why a disgruntled youth base gives rise to a restive [tense] nation."

Nigeria's youth have good reason to feel disgruntled and restive. Some even express hopelessness. According to the Nigerian Constitution, "Government shall direct its policy toward ensuring that there are equal and adequate educational opportunities at all levels." But little progress has been made toward such goals.

According to an opinion expressed in the Lagos newspaper *Daily Champion*, "a critical handicap in promoting youth affairs in [Nigeria] is the lack of credible role models among the older generation."

level, there are about 35 students for every available teacher. As full as they may be, classes go on, and the students continue to show up.

Nigerian education is based on a 6-3-3-4 system. This means children attend primary school for six years, beginning at the age of 6. At age 12, they leave primary school for the new experience of secondary school. Their first three years are called junior secondary school (JSS), and the last three years are senior secondary school (SSS). The final four years of the 6-3-3-4 system refer to a university education, but very few students get this far.

A student who manages to get a university diploma may be lucky to even find a job in his or her chosen field. Throughout the country, there are not enough jobs for all the qualified candidates. The alternatives are usually unemployment or leaving the country to find work—if the money to leave is available.

Students listen intently to the daily lesson despite being packed into an overcrowded classroom.

British-based Education

For some Nigerian teens, going to school means walking down a dusty village road to a one-room hut made of mud or concrete bricks. Others, especially in urban areas, attend impressive old schools made of stone and built in a Western architectural style. Most attend schools that are somewhere in between. Many of the schools that offer a more traditionally Western-style curriculum were constructed decades earlier by the English. (Nigeria was a British colony until gaining its independence in 1960.) The colonizers' early influence extends to the way schools are run as well. The Nigerian school system is based on the British model.

English, the official language of the country, is an important part of the curriculum. Altogether, 394 different languages are spoken in Nigeria, but Hausa, Igbo, and Yoruba are the major national languages. For the first three years of primary school, children learn in their native language, whatever it may be. From then on, all students learn in English.

The school year consists of three terms over 10 months. Years ago most secondary schools were boarding schools, but today about half of the students

For some Nigerian teens, a school day is spent entirely in an outdoor classroom.

are day students—they live with their families, returning home at the end of each day. Some secondary schools call themselves high schools. Others, following British tradition, are named colleges, such as St. Andrews College of Education. Many of them are Catholic or other religion-based institutions.

Uniforms are required in most schools. For younger boys, this usually means shorts—often khaki colored—and white shirts. Older boys also wear white shirts, but at age 12, they begin wearing long pants, most often black or navy. Girls usually wear simple solid-colored skirts and cotton blouses. In more old-fashioned schools, they wear berets and pinafores, aprons worn over dresses. Some schools also insist that girls, as well as boys, cut their hair extremely short. This is mainly to maintain a neat and tidy appearance among students and to discourage girls from spending hours braiding or styling their hair.

School Rules

At one Nigerian senior secondary school for girls, dress rules are clear-cut. They are also typical of many schools across the nation. A few of these include:
- Sandals must be brown. No slippers, covered shoes, or high heels are allowed.
- Hair braids must number 10 or more.
- Only SSS3 students (final year of senior secondary) are allowed to thread their hair.
- Only green and gold earrings are allowed.
- No dangling earrings are allowed.
- No rings, necklaces, rubber bands, or bangles are allowed.
- No makeup is allowed.
- No miniskirts or slit skirts are allowed.

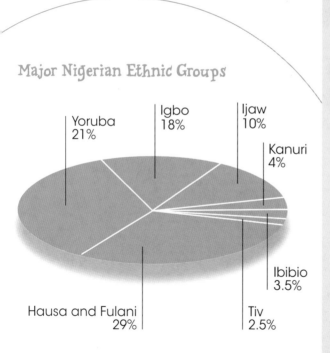

Major Nigerian Ethnic Groups

Yoruba 21%
Igbo 18%
Ijaw 10%
Kanuri 4%
Ibibio 3.5%
Hausa and Fulani 29%
Tiv 2.5%

Source: United States Central Intelligence Agency.
The World Factbook—Nigeria.

In areas where public transportation is not available, teens may have to walk several miles to reach their school.

North Versus South

The sweltering heat rising from the dusty streets of Kano, the capital of Kano state in northern Nigeria, does not slow Nigerians from their everyday activities. Men in long white robes and white knit caps called *tajia* pass noiselessly down twisted alleyways, while boys lead camels through the city's busy market. Workers squat in front of their open dye pits, dying fabric a rich indigo blue. Inside a mosque at the center of

tajia
tah-jee-YAH

town, though, the hushed air is cooler. There a group of students sit on intricately designed carpets, dedicating their time to their studies. The mosque is the place of worship for these Muslim teens and their families, but it is also their school. After morning prayers, the students—all young men—spend time reading and studying the Qur'an, the holy book of Islam.

About 50 percent of Nigeria's population is Muslim, and most Muslims are either Hausa or Fulani. The majority of them live in the vast northern one-third of the country, which is bounded on the south by two major rivers. Flowing from the northwest toward the center of the country is the Niger, the third-largest river in Africa. The Benue River runs from the northeast to merge into the Niger at Lokoja, in Nigeria's heartland. From there, the Niger flows straight south into the Gulf of Guinea and the Atlantic Ocean. The Y shape that these two rivers create separates the country into three major areas: the north, the southwest, and the southeast.

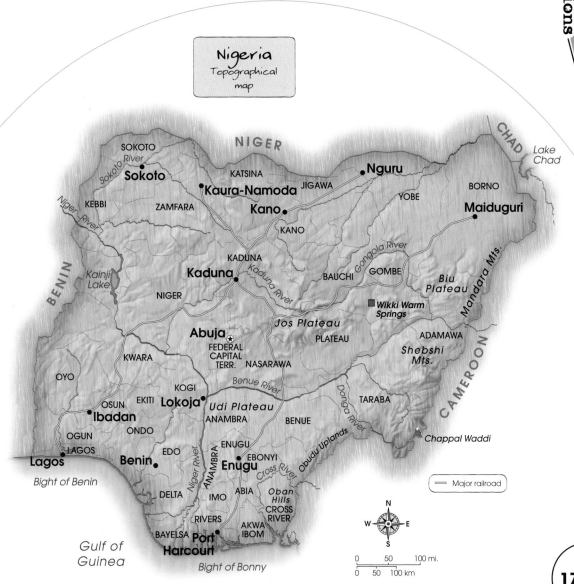

Nigeria
Topographical
map

NIGER
CHAD
Lake Chad
SOKOTO
Sokoto River
Sokoto
KATSINA
JIGAWA
Nguru
BORNO
KEBBI
Kaura-Namoda
ZAMFARA
Kano
YOBE
Maiduguri
Niger River
KANO
Gongola River
KADUNA
BAUCHI
GOMBE
Biu Plateau
Mandara Mts.
Kainji Lake
BENIN
Kaduna
Kaduna River
Wikki Warm Springs
NIGER
Jos Plateau
PLATEAU
ADAMAWA
Abuja
FEDERAL CAPITAL TERR.
NASARAWA
Shebshi Mts.
CAMEROON
KWARA
Benue River
OYO
KOGI
Donga River
TARABA
OSUN
EKITI
Lokoja
Udi Plateau
Ibadan
ONDO
ANAMBRA
BENUE
Obudu Uplands
OGUN
Chappal Waddi
LAGOS
EDO
ENUGU
Lagos
Benin
Niger River
EBONYI
Enugu
Cross River
Bight of Benin
Major railroad
DELTA
IMO
ABIA
Oban Hills
CROSS RIVER
RIVERS
AKWA IBOM
BAYELSA
Port Harcourt
N
W   E
S
Gulf of Guinea
Bight of Bonny
0   50   100 mi.
0   50   100 km

ATLANTIC OCEAN

Like the north, the southwestern and the southeastern portions are each dominated by a major ethnic group—Yoruba in the southwest and Igbo in the southeast. About half of the large Yoruba population is Muslim, and the other half is Christian. Other Christian groups, which make up 40 percent of the population, include the Igbo and most of the other ethnic groups who live in the south. The other 10 percent of the population—whether Yoruba, Igbo, Hausa, Fulani, or one of the countless other ethnic groups—practice traditional religions or a combination of these with either Christianity or Islam.

For the Hausa-Fulani in Nigeria's north, Islam is the guiding force in everyday living, especially education. Although secular, or nonreligion-based, Western-style schools are becoming more numerous in the north, there are not nearly as many in the southeast and southwest regions of the country. Traditionally, Muslim students are taught by a *mallam*, or Muslim scholar. Their Islamic education focuses primarily on reading and writing Arabic, the language of the Qur'an, and learning to recite passages from the holy book that are frequently used in prayer.

Some mallams strongly discourage Muslim parents from sending their

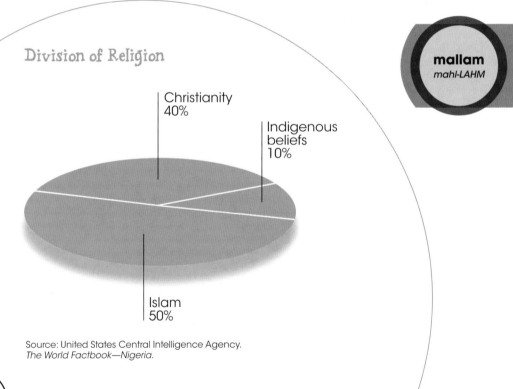

Division of Religion

Christianity
40%

Indigenous
beliefs
10%

Islam
50%

Source: United States Central Intelligence Agency.
The World Factbook—Nigeria.

mallam
mahl-LAHM

children to schools that are not traditionally Islamic. Many parents and other adults, Muslims in particular, feel that public education in Nigeria is undisciplined and fails to provide the high moral standards that a religious education would provide.

Transcribing the Qur'an is a typical lesson for Muslims.

Educating the "Girl Child"

Nigerian attitudes toward educating girls are changing—slowly. In Bauchi state, in northern Nigeria, the government has passed a progressive Girl Child Education Bill. This bill is meant to help girls stay in school until they have finished the entire six years of secondary school. It pays tuition and examination fees for girls whose parents cannot afford these expenses.

Ever larger numbers of girls are beginning to get the education they deserve. As of 2004, for every 100 boys in primary and secondary school, there were 84 girls enrolled. In the north, the number of enrolled girls is far less.

Many Muslims see no reason to send girls to school, especially after primary school, because they are expected to marry young. Similarly, in many other ethnic cultures, the value of educating girls is just beginning to be recognized.

Overall, traditional Western-style, secular education is much more common in the southeastern and southwestern regions of the country. In many cases, the lack of education in the

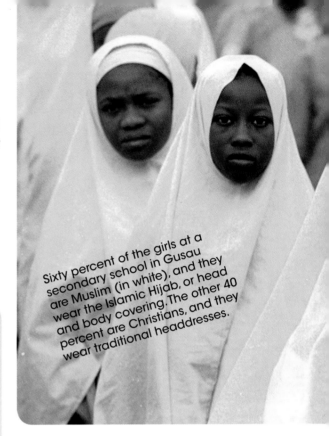

Sixty percent of the girls at a secondary school in Gusau are Muslim (in white), and they wear the Islamic Hijab, or head and body covering. The other 40 percent are Christians, and they wear traditional headdresses.

States Under Sharia

Nineteen of Nigeria's northern states are under sharia law, which dictates a strict Islamic code of behavior. People living in these states are forbidden from viewing movies, drinking alcoholic beverages, and mixing with the opposite sex. Punishment for criminals is harsh, including amputation and stoning. This has led to turmoil and even rioting by Christians who live in these states and consider sharia unconstitutional. But those in favor of it believe it is the only way to counteract what they see as Nigeria's massive corruption, crime, and poverty.

north widens the deep divide between the north and the south and between Muslims and Christians. The struggle of these two major religions to coexist has given rise to severe ethnic and religious conflict, especially in the north.

Strict Rules & Heavy Course Loads

Although the quality of education is not at the level many Nigerians feel it needs to be, the Nigerian government has done much in recent years to standardize education. It has allotted more money to building and improving school structures and hiring and training

teachers. It has also set basic educational requirements for all students nationwide, and it is making efforts to improve and standardize textbooks. Over the past few decades, literacy has greatly increased. As of 2002, 91 percent of Nigerian males between 15 and 24 years old could read and write. And 87 percent of females in the same age range were also literate.

To keep the literacy rate up, Nigerian secondary school students have tough schedules. They typically carry heavy course loads, taking as many as 11 or 12 different courses per term. Additionally, rules are strict, and the discipline is harsh.

By law, students are only required to finish JSS. This will give them both academic and prevocational knowledge. Some of the many courses required of students ages 12 through 14 are two native Nigerian languages, math,

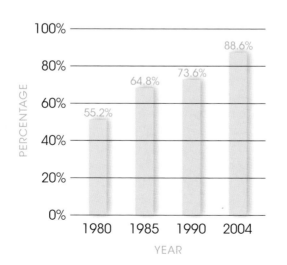

Growth of Literacy

Source: Globalis—Nigeria.

social studies, physical education, agricultural science, religious studies, and English. They also take two pre-vocational subjects, such as local crafts, home economics, or metalworking.

Students who successfully pass their final JSS exams are awarded the Junior School Certificate. From there, if they choose to continue their education, they can stream into one of three different tracks. Their choice will be determined by their abilities, interests, and test results. Of JSS graduates, only 34 percent go on to the next level.

Of those, 60 percent will enter senior secondary school. Twenty percent enroll in technical college (equivalent to vocational high school). The other 20 percent are divided equally among apprenticeship programs, such as carpentry, and vocational training centers.

Secondary school students take six core subjects and two or three electives. The core curriculum includes English, math, a vocational subject, and a major Nigerian language—Igbo, Yoruba, Hausa, or the language of their own ethnic group. Depending on what year

Corporal Punishment

Another legacy of the British Empire that Nigeria's schools have inherited is corporal punishment—the use of physical pain to change behavior. When teens disobey the rules and regulations, punishment can be harsh and swift. In many schools, beatings—commonly called lashings, canings, or floggings—are not unusual. Another common punishment is being forced to kneel, sometimes for several hours and occasionally on hot sand or stones. A student may also be suspended or expelled for fighting with others or bringing sharp weapons to school.

Some lesser punishments include being assigned to clean classrooms or toilets, helping with jobs on the school grounds, or, in schools that have no running water, going to fetch water from a river or stream, some of which may be miles away.

A School Day

Not all Nigerian schools follow the same schedule, but many are similar. Whether a boarding school or day student, a teen's school day often looks like this:

5:30 or 6:00 A.M.	Get up and do chores around the house or at school
6:30 A.M.	Wash and dress
7:00 A.M.	Breakfast
7:30 or 8:00 A.M.	Classes begin
2:00 P.M.	Lunch
3:00 P.M.	Rest period
4:00 P.M.	Sports/physical education
5:00 P.M.	Chores around the house, especially for girls
6:00 P.M.	Dinner
7:00 P.M.	Study/homework; students in boarding school must return to their classroom for this study period—they may not talk or leave the room
9:30 P.M.	Get ready for bed
10:00 P.M.	Lights out

they are in, they will also take biology, chemistry, physics, or integrated science. They take courses in English literature, history, geography, or social studies as well. The long list of electives include choices as varied as building construction, clothing and textile history, Bible knowledge, and Islamic studies.

One course that does not appear on the curriculum is drivers' education. Although teens may apply for a driver's license at 18, only 4.9 percent of Nigeria's population owns cars. Another 10.2 percent drive motorcycles.

At the end of senior secondary school, students take further exams. If they pass, they will receive their Senior School Certificate. From there, a student may go on to the tertiary level, or university. Others may opt for military service. Teens can legally enlist at the age of 18.

Along the way, from primary

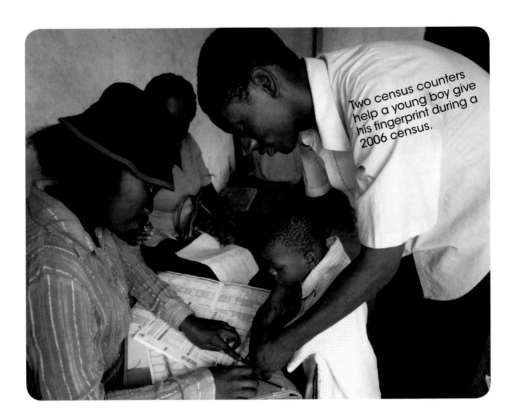

Two census counters help a young boy give his fingerprint during a 2006 census.

school to the end of SSS, many will have dropped out. In 2006, Nigeria attempted its first census in 15 years, so the dropout rates have been difficult to measure. But some of the reasons for dropping out are well known. These include parents removing students for marriage (mainly girls) or apprenticeships (mainly boys) or because of financial reasons. Many students leave for these same reasons of their own accord.

A recent study found that 25 percent of students said they had been removed from school because their parents had no interest in education. For a variety of reasons, some Nigerians do not recognize the value of school. More than 6 million school-age Nigerian children are not being educated.

Although many throughout the country urgently feel that a solid education is the most crucial step toward healing the country's ills, they also see the government doing little about it. Nigerian schools have many problems yet to be solved. Supplies of all kinds, especially textbooks, are not even available in many rural schools. Those that do exist—in any school—may have to be shared by several students. They often are printed on low-quality paper, contain outdated material, and are badly designed.

A perhaps more serious problem is corruption related to grades and exam results. In a country where bribery is often considered normal business, some parents use money to help their children get ahead. School and testing officials are sometimes bribed to award higher grades or test scores to the children of parents who pay.

Nigerian native Dr. Ogbu Kalu, a professor at McCormick Theological Seminary in the United States, is deeply troubled by what he observes on his return visits to his homeland. He noted that throughout the country, thousands of youths are "hanging around doing nothing." Unable to afford school and with no jobs available to them, there is nothing left to do. "We are watching generations as they waste," Kalu commented, "and the nation will pay a terrible price for its neglect."

Despite education problems in Nigeria, the student population at the University of Lagos grew from 131 in 1962 to more than 39,000 in 2006.

Because many Nigerian homes consist of a single room, the family members must share living and sleeping quarters.

2 Life at Home

AS NIGHT FALLS ACROSS NIGERIA, FAMILIES GATHER TOGETHER FOR THEIR EVENING MEAL. Whether they live in the most remote villages, in medium-size towns, or in cities with populations of millions, Nigerian families are close-knit. The family unit is the center of their social lives, and coming together to share meals is a highlight of that socializing.

In a typical household, every meal includes plenty of hot, spicy food. Pepper soup, pounded yam, plaintains, thick meat stews, and jollof rice are common dishes. Foods are spiced up with red chilies, ground peppercorns, garlic, and ginger. After dinner, there

may be singing, dancing, drumming, and storytelling. Until recently, Nigeria's history, customs, and traditions have mostly been passed down orally. The past comes alive as the elders share stories and legends about the origins of their people.

Because of their age, wisdom, and many years of experience, older people always hold a position of high status within the community. Young people are taught that their parents are the source of their lives and should be treated with the greatest respect. Much of this respect also comes from the fact that the parents have worked hard and sacrificed in many ways for their children.

Mmm-mmm Good

Eating together is an important part of Nigerian daily life, and Nigerian food offers a feast of flavors. Diet basics include rice, beans, yams, corn, millet, and cassava, a root vegetable that is the source of tapioca. Plaintains are similar to bananas but must be cooked before eating. Thick, red palm oil is an important ingredient in many dishes, and peanuts are also frequently used. For those who can afford it, meats such as chicken, goat, and beef are included in many dishes. Hunters may bring home "bush meat," or wild game.

For drinks, adults might have palm wine or beer, often made from maize or even bananas or sugarcane. Teens such as "minerals"—soda drinks in flavors like Afri-Cola, Mirinda (mandarin orange), and Zit (citrus).

Another popular traditional dish in Nigeria is goat's head soup. The soup pot for this recipe contains just about every part of the goat—including the bones, eyes, ears, and tongue.

A typical daily menu might include:

Breakfast	Lunch	Dinner
pap (a porridge made from the cereal grain maize), fried plantains, and eggs; tea and coffee are popular drinks, especially in the city	pepper soup with some meat or fish in broth; garri, or cassava dough, is dipped in the soup and eaten by hand	a thick soup or stew made with some kind of meat or fish and local vegetables, such as pumpkin leaf or ukazi leaf; it's accompanied by spicy jollof rice, cooked with tomatoes and onions; chin-chin is a dessert made from fried strips of pastry dough.

chin-chin
CHIN-chin

In Nigerian society, it is still a strong custom for teens to honor their parents by prostrating themselves—lying face down or bowing low before them.

Respect for parents and many common ties unite the people of this nation. But in the opinion of one young Nigerian journalist, not all that comes from the elders is wisdom. He says,

"Sometimes myopic [narrow-minded] social, political, and religious elders control either the level of exposure of the youth or their interpretation of the facts and figures from inside and outside the country. As a direct result, Nigerian youth are probably more confused than they ought to be about what they should be doing, eating, watching, wearing. … They are often left to their own devices."

Many factors determine how Nigerian teens live on a day-to-day basis. Lifestyle is greatly determined by the ethnic group and religion one belongs to and the wealth of one's family. There are also many differences between the lives of rural teens and those living in cities and larger towns. While some of these are slight differences, others are major.

Life in a Nigerian City

Today, Nigeria's urban areas are overflowing with people who have migrated from the rural regions looking for jobs and a better way of life. They have good reason to be drawn to these places. Lagos, Ibadan, Jos, and other big cities are sophisticated urban centers. They

Mealtime Customs, Hausa Style

As Muslims, most Hausa men and boys eat separately from the women and girls in a different part of the house. Meals are served in a large dish that all the diners eat from while seated on the floor.

To walk around or even stand while eating is considered "eating with the devil." The Hausa believe that the act of eating must be done respectfully because food sustains life. Eating with the left hand is strictly forbidden, as are many topics of conversation, such as clothing, livestock, or even complimenting the food. These things are considered *santi*, a violation of proper behavior. Unlike in Western society, a good, loud burp at the dinner table is not

santi
sahn-TEE

considered rude. Rather, in most parts of Africa and the Middle East, it indicates a great appreciation for the meal. It's always a compliment to the chef's cooking when someone belches loudly during and after eating.

have an international flavor and links to the rest of the world. They are exciting, dynamic, and full of opportunities.

The small percentage of urban families with high incomes especially benefit from the advantages the cities offer. They may own a comfortably furnished home, whereas almost 70 percent of Nigerian families live in single-room dwellings. A few may be part of the mere 1.5 percent of Nigerians who have the luxury of a landline

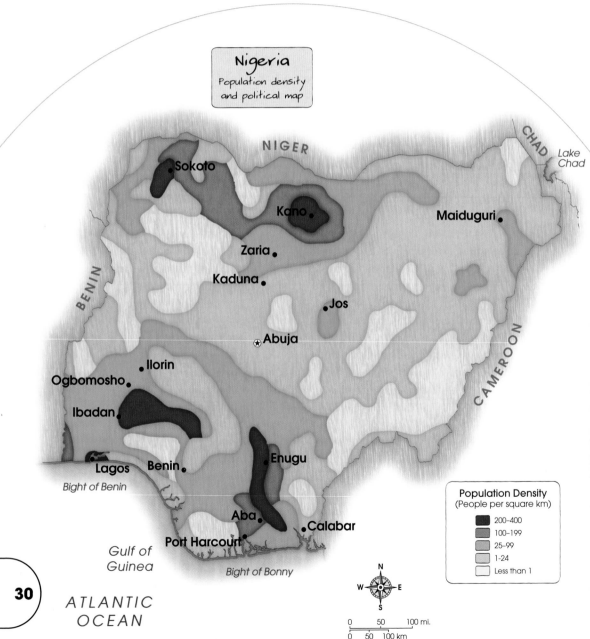

Nigeria
Population density
and political map

NIGER

CHAD
Lake Chad

Sokoto

Kano

Maiduguri

Zaria

BENIN

Kaduna

Jos

Abuja

Ilorin

CAMEROON

Ogbomosho

Ibadan

Lagos   Benin

Enugu

Bight of Benin

Aba

Calabar

Port Harcourt

Gulf of Guinea

Bight of Bonny

Population Density
(People per square km)

■	200–400
■	100–199
■	25–99
■	1–24
□	Less than 1

N
W   E
S

ATLANTIC OCEAN

0   50   100 mi.
0   50   100 km

telephone. More will have running water, something only 19.6 percent of the nation's households have. Even then, if it is pumped in by electricity, water may be available only a few hours a day. When it is, families try to fill large buckets and tubs so that they will still have water once it is shut off again.

Despite these inconveniences, most modern, middle- and upper-income Nigerian teens have a relatively easy life. But they represent only a small portion of the nation's population. Most Nigerians live a dramatically different lifestyle in grinding poverty. About 92 percent of the population lives on about 267 naira ($U.S.2) a day. The urban areas also face huge problems with

crime, drugs, and AIDS.

That means, for the less fortunate, city life can be brutal. Hundreds of thousands of people end up in over-crowded shantytowns on the fringes of cities. Low-income families may make their homes in mud shacks or open-sided lean-tos on the edges of dusty, unpaved streets. Even if a family is lucky enough to have more than one room, Nigerian families are typically large. A teen may end up sharing sleeping space on the dirt floor with numerous siblings or even the whole family.

A fortunate poor family might have a tin roof overhead. A meal may be a piece of bread, a few spoonfuls of rice or beans, or whatever can be found to

Stilt houses are constructed in the water to accomodate the population surge in Nigeria's cities.

eat by begging or scavenging in one of the heaping mounds of garbage that dot some cities.

Life in a Nigerian Village

Under the conditions existing in many village societies, daily life for most teens involves a lot of chores and perhaps little schooling. Simple daily life takes extra effort. In villages where there is no running water, many people spend one to three hours a day just bringing water home for drinking and cooking. Some villages have wells dug deep in the earth, and the water can be pumped by hand. Where the land is too hard for digging, water must be carried in from rivers or springs. Often these sources are several hundred yards, or even miles, away. Sometimes trucks bring water for sale.

As well as scarce running water, electricity is rarely available in villages. Throughout Nigeria, almost 40 percent of homes have none at all. A fortunate family might have its own generator, but kerosene is the fuel most used for light. Also, because they have no gas, electricity, or coal for cooking and heat, almost three-quarters of the population rely on wood for these things.

Girls are expected to be resourceful, modest, hard-working, and always graceful and obedient under pressure. They are trained from a young age to master all the skills needed to run a household and raise children. Village girls may cook, clean, sweep, and wash clothes. They will be expected to watch their younger siblings, gather firewood, and, of course, fetch water. They also frequently accompany their mothers to the local open-air market, both to shop and sell goods of their own.

Nigerians girls cross a highway with lumber piled high on their backs.

Teen Scene

In rural Nigeria, a girl strolls down the main road of her village. On either side of the road, tall reeds grow, partially sheltering from view the buildings behind them. She wears a white cotton blouse and a colorful "wrapper," a long piece of print fabric wrapped around her waist. She walks gracefully in her flip-flops, expertly balancing on her head a large, dried calabash gourd filled with fresh water.

The girl turns through an opening in the wall of reeds and suddenly she is home. Chicken and goats run freely around the family compound. They may be pets for the time being, but they will most likely end up as part of a meal.

The girl's family's compound consists of a number of round huts with cone-shaped thatch roofs. A wide-open courtyard serves as an outdoor living room. Cooking is often done here too.

Bringing water home is only one of this girl's many chores. She is expected to help her mother with every aspect of running the household. This work, begun at a young age, early marriage, and an unchanging rural life may be all her future holds.

Far from the village, in a bustling Nigerian city, a boy wakes at 6 o'clock to get ready for another school day. He is lucky this morning—when he turns on the shower, water flows. After bathing, the boy dresses in his school uniform. When he is not in school, he usually wears clothing with Western brand names. He does not receive an allowance, but he does get spending money for school meals and other necessities.

After a family breakfast of porridge, coffee, and toast, the boy's parents go off to their full-time, white-collar jobs. Although they cannot afford to own their comfortably furnished home, they do have the luxury of a driver who takes the boy to his private school each day. Most students will get there by bus or taxi, or on foot.

If the boy stays in school, he may very well go on to college. But it is highly uncertain that a job will be available to him in his homeland once he graduates.

No Running Water

The lack of clean water is a major problem in Nigeria. One of the biggest drawbacks of having no running water is that it means having no indoor plumbing. Toilet facilities vary dramatically from village to town to city. But most are unsanitary, if not hazardous. Fewer than 10 percent of Nigerian homes have modern bathroom facilities. The other 90 percent of the population use covered pits. In some cases, uncovered pits, rivers and streams, or latrine pails are the only things available.

During a water shortage in Nigeria, a Lagos citizen provides water from a tanker for a penny per pail.

Building a well in the middle of a town is a community effort that saves many hours a day transporting water.

Teen boys have plenty of chores too, but their tasks rarely involve anything considered "women's work." Traditional ideas about the proper roles of men and women are still strongly embedded in the culture. Boys also generally have much more leisure time than girls do.

No matter where they live, Nigerian teens have their work cut out for them. But village teens may be at a greater disadvantage. Even villagers who are better off may not have a nearby school to send their children to. And there are not the kinds of job opportunities available in cities. With little access to education or decent work, young Nigerians have few opportunities to change their circumstances.

Following a long-standing tradition, Nigerian girls learn to balance and transport heavy items on their heads at a young age.

3

Major Milestones

MEMBERS OF A NIGERIAN FAMILY, AS WELL AS CLOSE FRIENDS, GATHER FOR MANY IMPORTANT CERE-MONIES. One of the most important is the day that a family's new baby will be named. It is a formal occasion of celebration and joy.

Virtually all of Nigeria's ethnic groups engage in naming ceremonies for their newborns. Each occurs in a different way, following traditions passed down over centuries. For the Hausa, the ceremony takes place on the seventh day of the infant's life. For the Igbo, formal naming usually occurs on the 28th day. Yoruba babies are kept inside the house with their mothers, and neither is seen publicly until the naming ceremony. For girls, this takes place at six days and for boys at eight days. No matter how the ceremony unfolds, it is the first important milestone in the life of a young Nigerian.

Another important milestone will be the wedding ceremony. And for most Nigerian youth, the years between the naming ceremony and the wedding are few.

A Yoruba wedding ceremony draws relatives from all over Nigeria.

Traditional values require that people marry early and begin raising a family. Single adults have little place within most ethnic societies, which hold to age-old customs and beliefs. Unmarried people are often looked upon with suspicion or sometimes even driven from the community.

Another long-standing national custom is polygyny, the practice of having more than one wife. Although it is becoming less common today, especially in urban areas, polygyny is still widely practiced. Those who practice traditional religions may have as many wives as they can afford to support. In the past, Nigerian kings sometimes had hundreds of wives. Today men who practice polygyny marry fewer wives. Muslims may have up to four wives. Even some Christians, who by the rules of the church are supposed to have only one wife, may nevertheless be polygynysts. In most cases, multiple wives and many children would mean too many mouths to feed and too many children to educate. Once, most women had an average of seven children; today the average is about five.

With a male head of household, several wives, and children—as well as relatives that include multiple grandparents, aunts, uncles, and cousins—the extended family is often extremely large. In rural areas, members of such an extended family usually live near one another or together in a large family compound. The compound often has separate sleeping quarters for the head of the household and any older sons he may have. Each wife typically has her own living space, where her daughters and younger sons live with her. Additional buildings within the compound house the other relatives. Most of these people will see young family members through the rites and rituals that are part of their ethnic heritage.

Naming Ceremonies in Many Flavors

Like the baby itself, the maternal grandmother is at the center of an Igbo naming ceremony. She cooks the food for the feast that begins the ceremony. When the baby is brought in, the grandmother is first to suggest a name for the baby. Then the parents and guests also offer their suggestions. When the festive event ends, the guests leave gifts and money for the grandmother as well as the child. The parents then take time to consider all the name suggestions before choosing the one they like best.

Among the Yoruba, the naming ceremony is detailed and elaborate. A baby's name is never chosen before birth. The oldest member of the family performs the ritual, using many ceremonial items. Water signifies that the child is important to the family, because water is precious. Honey represents the wish that the child be sweet and a help to his or her community. A tiny bit of ginger,

symbolizing good health, may be given to the infant to taste. Other elements that may also be used include kola nuts, palm oil, sugar, wine, and salt. If a coin or other money is held up to the baby, and he or she reaches for it, the Yoruba believe this indicates future prosperity. For Christians or Muslims, it may also symbolize the parents' hope that their child never loves anything more than God.

A grandmother and grandchild are at the center of attention during a naming ceremony.

What's in a Name

Babies are especially well loved in Nigeria. Traditionally they are considered a blessing for the family. When they are older, they can help provide financially for the family. Because Nigeria does not have health insurance or retirement communities, children are expected to take care of their aging parents. So the inability to have children is seen as one of the most unfortunate things that could happen to a married couple.

Nigerians believe that a name has a great influence on a child's future. Most babies receive at least three names—one from the father, one from the mother, and one usually from an older relative. In Christian families especially, a child will receive not only traditional names, but a Christian name as well.

Some typical Yoruba names and their meanings:

Olusegun—God has conquered the enemy

Tayewo—the taster of the world

Ayoke (female)—one whom people are happy to bless

Abike (female)—one who is born to be pampered

Some typical Igbo names and their meanings:

Nneka (female)—mother is supreme

Adaobi (female)—daughter of the family

Udodi—there is peace

Nwakaego—a child is better than money

Ngozi—blessing

Ifeanyicukwu—God is almighty

Some typical Muslim boy names:

Kabir

Ibrahim

Habibu

Saddam

Abubakir

Some typical Muslim girl names:

Kamila

Khadeeja

Khansa

Qahira

Qudsia

When guests arrive for a Hausa naming ceremony, the father offers them kola nuts, a gesture of hospitality. A mallam from the community leads prayers for the child. During this time, an animal, usually a ram or a bull, is sacrificed. The father has the final say on what the child's name will be, whether his wife agrees or not. At the end of the ceremony, a barber shaves the child's head, and if the father wishes, marks its head with tribal tattoos.

In Between Being Named & Being Wed

In a Hausa household, when a young man reaches puberty, his life is about to change in an important way. As children, boys run freely into the homes of friends, playing with girls as well as boys. At that age, boys can spend time with their young sisters, casually enjoying their company.

Eventually the lives of Hausa boys and girls go in separate directions. When they reach about 10 to 12 years of age, their childhood years are considered over. By tradition, they are now adults. Boys, who could once move freely from the men's to the women's quarters, will now have to stay far from all women, except perhaps their closest relatives.

The abrupt loss of the freedom of childhood is especially extreme for girls. In the strictest households, when a girl reaches 10 or 12, she must begin preparing herself for marriage. As part of this preparation, she enters *purdah*. According to this Islamic custom, she is now confined to the hidden life behind the walls of the family compound. Her society becomes only the other females in her household. From now on, she will rarely see any men except those in her immediate family. For many young teen girls, this transition is a difficult one.

purdah
per-DAH

Boys, too, must soon begin to think about marriage. It is taken for granted that young people will marry, and until recently, girls especially have had few other options. A boy has a few years to accumulate "bride wealth," money and other property that is given to the girl's father. This proves to the parents of his intended bride that he can properly support her. Boys generally are not expected to marry before the age of 20. A girl must also store up material goods to show she comes from a family of good standing. Most girls will marry long before most boys do, sometimes as early as age 10.

Many non-Muslim ethnic groups also have rigid rules that dictate how and when teens of the opposite sex can share each other's company. But things are often looser for non-Muslim teens.

Dating among teens is rare in any ethnic group because so much time is spent on school or work, or both. Strict moral values add further pressure

Early to the Altar

All Nigerian cultures have songs for the special milestones of life, such as birthdays, weddings, and deaths. The Igbo culture also includes maternity songs, which emphasize that a girl's worth comes from being married. A typical one of these songs includes the lyrics "Be you as beautiful as a mermaid, the beauty of a woman is to have a husband." At birth, baby girls in that culture may be spoken of as being an *obute aku* ("source of wealth") or an *akpa-ego* ("bag of money"). These expressions refer to the money and other positive things that will come from marriage. This custom of marrying girls off early is hard to break. But today many progressive Nigerian women and men are actively involved in changing attitudes that are harmful to women and girls.

obute aku
oh-boo-TEH ah-COO

akpa-ego
ahk-PAH-eh-GO

to focus on other things, especially in the north. Nigeria's AIDS crisis keeps informed teens from wanting to get intimate before marriage as well. But abstinence is not emphasized nearly as much in the south.

Among more modern-thinking families, and in cities where there are greater numbers of educated people, old rules about behavior generally have

Hoping to make teens aware of the AIDS crisis, an HIV-positive educator conducts a workshop for teachers in Lagos.

less influence. Teens have more oppor-tunities to spend time with members of the opposite sex. This is especially true in the less religion-dominated southern region of Nigeria. There young people with goals of graduating from college and pursuing a career are putting off marriage much longer than the earlier generations did.

Marriage at a Young Age

In a nomadic Fulani tribe, two young women who are both teens and close in age may look similar. But even from afar, anyone familiar with Fulani cus-toms can tell whether they are married. The clues are mainly in the way they wear their hair.

A Fulani woman's hairstyle reveals much about her background and social

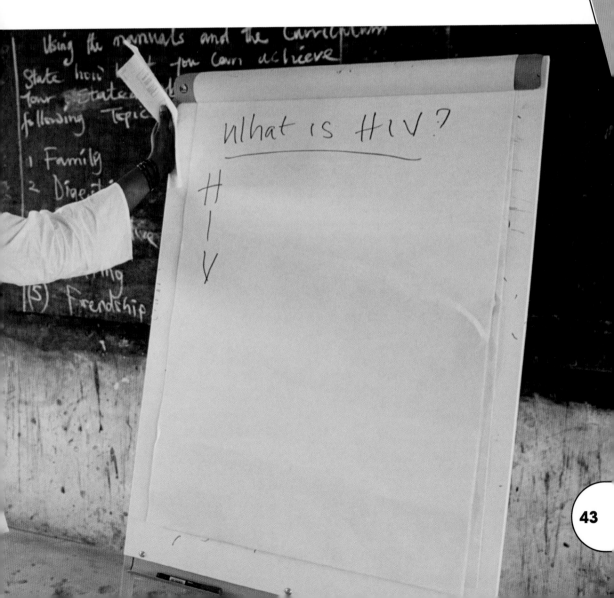

AIDS Crisis

HIV and AIDS have reached epidemic proportions throughout Africa, where it is the most common cause of death. The situation is not as extreme in Nigeria as in some other countries on the continent, but the picture is still grim. Life expectancy there is about 47 years, and it may be decreasing because of AIDS deaths. A 2003 survey showed that about 3.3 million Nigerians were living with HIV or AIDS, an estimate that is likely much lower than the actual number of people infected. Most of those carrying the virus are teenagers and people in their 20s. A majority of these are girls.

Traditionally, sex has been a taboo subject among some Nigerian cultures, especially in the north. As a result, these young people never learn how to protect themselves. Making the problem worse is the fact that there is no legal age for marriage. Young, uninformed girls become the wives of older men, who have multiple sexual partners. This often leads to the teenage wives becoming infected with HIV, which they may in turn pass on to their babies in the womb.

At a volunteer counseling and testing center in Abuja, a medical lab scientist checks samples of blood for HIV and AIDS.

status. One girl's hair may be decorated with extremely large pieces of amber, and she wears heavy gold earrings that hang nearly to her shoulders and look like thick slices of melon. These lavish adornments signal that she is married, most likely to a prosperous man.

Another girl may have many silver coins and small amber beads woven into her hair. Until they marry, girls use only small beads and coins in their hair.

Typically, especially in Muslim societies, who and when a girl marries are almost always entirely arranged by her parents. The bride-to-be has little choice in the matter. For the Fulani, the husband should be someone belonging to the same bloodline, or clan. The ideal mate is a first cousin. Among the Yoruba and Igbo, marrying relatives is strictly forbidden.

A single woman displays her marital status by decorating her hair with small beads and coins.

Because the vast majority of Igbo are Christians, most have a church wedding, including a white wedding dress, a procession down the aisle, and an exchange of vows and rings. At the reception, many newlywed couples wear traditional Nigerian dress. Some young couples have two ceremonies. Besides the Christian ceremony, they marry in the way that is customary to their particular ethnic group. Since the Yoruba population is split between Islam and Christianity, the ceremony depends on each couple's religion.

Among some ethnic groups, and in the most remote areas, the influence of modern life has barely been felt. But modern ways are gradually being accepted. According to Ghaji Badawi, a professor at Nigeria's Beyero University, "Families are becoming smaller and smaller. They're changing from extended families to the nuclear family."

The conflict between old and new is likely to cause dramatic changes in the lives of many—especially Nigeria's young people. As they grow up, marry, and raise their own families, however, some things will stay the same. The young will still identify strongly with the rites, rituals, and traditions they have been taught from birth. They will, in turn, introduce their children to many of the old practices, thereby keeping their culture alive.

A newly married bride and groom wear a wedding dress and tuxedo, while some of their older relatives don more traditional outfits that represent their tribe.

Dressing Up

When Nigerians dress up in their native styles, they create beautiful patterns with vibrant colors. Creative ways of using fabric give a bold sense of style. Traditional fabric designs are often a reflection of local culture.

Women and girls wear long wrappers in boldly colored fabrics. For dressy events, they may fashion matching rectangles of fabric into many styles of turbans or headties. Loose, free-flowing, cotton robes are common because of the heat. Menswear includes the agbada, a long, flowing robe worn for formal occasions by heads of state, and the dansiki, a loose, tunic-length robe that reaches the knees or the shins. Men and women both wear the boubou, a long, wide-sleeved robe. Men also wear tunics called bubas and sokoto, or loose, tapering pants. Many of the country's colorful costumes come from Lagos, Nigeria's fashion capital.

agbada
ahg-bah-DAH
dansiki
dahn-see-KEE
boubou
boh-BOH

bubas
boo-BAHS
sokoto
soh-koh-TOH

Traditional flutes called *zunguru* are blown during the Durbar festival in Kano.

4

A Time to Celebrate

ON OCTOBER 1, TEENS ARE NOWHERE NEAR THE CLASS-ROOM. Their clothes, which are bright and colorful, make them look anything but ready for school. Instead of school uniforms, a few wear tradi-tional Nigerian dress. The rest wear Western-style shirts and pants, or dresses, in varying combinations of bright green and white, the colors of the Nigerian flag. The green stands for the nation's rich agricultural wealth, and the white is a sym-bol of unity and peace.

Instead of going to school, teens make their way to a local stadium. But they will not be watching a sports match, and they are not ditching school. Throughout the country, schools and businesses are closed for the day because it is an important national holiday: Nigeria's Independence Day, sometimes called National Day or Republic Day.

On October 1, 1960, after 65 years of British colo-nial rule, Nigeria took control of its own fate. In every state, and especially in the Federal Capital Territory, located at the heart of the nation, National Day marks that transition to freedom with major festivities.

A hunter stalks his prey during a play highlighting a festival in Argungu.

Some towns and villages may come up with their own special ways of celebrating. But many civic celebrations with pomp and circumstance are modeled after those introduced by the British colonizers during the first half of the 20th century. This is particularly true in Abuja, the nation's capital city. Military parades mark the day.

Marching bands strut across the fields, stirring the crowds with their brass horns and drums. At some celebrations, students march as well, dressed in their school uniforms. Government leaders give patriotic speeches about Nigeria's past and its hopes for the future. Deserving students and others may receive awards.

National Holidays in Nigeria

When the formal National Day activities are over, people gather to celebrate with friends and family. Sometimes the parties last all night. In some cities, big movie premieres are scheduled. On lively occasions like these, Nigerians dress up and have fun!

New Year's Day is an equally festive national holiday that all Nigerians enjoy. For young students, these occasions mean a break from school and welcome changes to the everyday routine. In some Nigerian families, the new year is celebrated for two days. Many people stay up all night to see the new year in. They look ahead to new beginnings and fresh starts. Many teens receive presents or new clothes for New Year's, and good food is plentiful. Loud noisemakers and dancing are also part of the fun. Often families that have moved to the city return to the towns or villages they came from and enjoy reunions with relatives and friends.

Some of Nigeria's other national holidays include Workers Day on May 1 and Children's Day on May 27. These public holidays are celebrated by every citizen. But in a nation as complex, layered, and multiethnic as Nigeria, the year is filled with hundreds of other festivals, celebrations, and ceremonies, many held only in specific regions. Some of these events are religious. Others are specific to the cultures of individual ethnic groups.

Nigeria's festivals often feature dancing and colorful costumes.

A Year of Holidays

Nigerians celebrate a number of national holidays. Those with fixed dates include:

New Year's Day—January 1

Workers Day (or Labor Day)—May 1

Children's Day—May 27

National Day (or Independence Day)—October 1

Christmas—December 25

Boxing Day—December 26

Nigerians also celebrate many religious holidays that fall on different dates each year. Some of the most important are:

Eid-al-Kabir—A three- to four-day holiday celebrating the end of the Islamic year and honoring Abraham, an important ancient figure in the Muslim religion.

Good Friday—Celebrated in March or April, this Christian holiday commemorates the crucifixion of Jesus Christ.

Easter—Celebrated on the Sunday following Good Friday, this Christian holiday commemorates the resurrection of Jesus Christ.

Eid-al-Fitr—Celebration of the end of the Islamic month of Ramadan

The Delights of Christmas

In December, with Christmas on the way, many Nigerian cities empty out, especially in the southern and eastern regions, where the Christian members of the Igbo and Yoruba groups predominate. Everyone wants to be home for this most important Christian holiday of the year. When Christmas comes, schools and businesses close and everyone has time off, even those who do not celebrate the holiday. When the major Muslim holidays arrive, the same will be true.

Christmas in Nigeria combines worldwide traditions with those unique to Nigeria itself. It is a time of celebration, dance, and family warmth. Nigerian Christians are Catholic, as well as many other denominations, and long before Christmas Day arrives, church choirs begin rehearsing their holiday hymns. Some choirs go out caroling in the church neighborhood. Instead of decorating the traditional Christmas tree, teens often help decorate homes and churches with palm fronds, a symbol of peace. Sometimes the fronds are woven into wreaths.

Many Nigerian Catholics celebrate Christmas by attending Mass.

After midnight Mass on Christmas Eve or church on Christmas morning, the festivities get under way. Singing, dancing, and drumming are a lively part of the celebration, often in the town or village square. Boys construct masks using raffia, tough material from a palm tree, and other materials. Then they compete in colorful masquerades that involve drumming and dancing. Each hopes to win the prize for the best mask.

Christmas dinner is the finest feast a family can afford. If the money is there, a family may buy a live goat, ram, sheep, or some chickens for the occasion. On Christmas Day, these animals become the main dish on the dinner table. Turkey is rarely part of the meal because it must be imported and is therefore expensive. Traditional Nigerian dishes are also served. Guests eat thick goat stews, fried plantains, pounded yam, and spicy jollof rice made with lots of red pepper and tomato paste.

Ekon Play

The Ekon play is another unique Nigerian Christmas tradition. A group of colorfully dressed drummers, dancers, and actors stream through the neighborhoods. They go door-to-door to each family compound, carrying a special bundle—a doll that represents the baby Jesus. The people at home accept the doll, which represents blessings, and offer *dash*, or gifts, to the Ekon members. Then they return the baby Jesus, and the procession goes on its way to the next home.

dash
dahsh

Although presents are exchanged, toys are not usually a big part of the gift-giving. Teens are more likely to get new clothes and, sometimes, new shoes. Giving to the poor is also an important Christmas custom. Those who can afford it donate money or useful goods to less-fortunate members of the community. Others cook food. Everyone in the extended family is especially taken care of. In Nigeria, Christmas is a time of warm spirits and warm weather.

Ramadan & Eid-al-Fitr

The thinnest sliver of moon hangs low in the Nigerian night sky. The ninth month in the Islamic calendar, Ramadan, has officially begun with the sighting of this new moon. During Ramadan especially, Muslim teens, like all followers of Islam, are called to turn their minds and hearts more fully to Allah, or God. To help them do so, they will spend the entire month fasting—neither eating nor drinking anything—from dawn to dusk every day. Although young people are not required to participate in the fast until they reach puberty, many do. By fasting, they hope to experience a closer connection to Allah.

The Islamic calendar is based on the cycles of the moon, so the beginning of Ramadan falls on a different date each year. During this month, teens and their elders are expected to pay greater attention to being good. This means letting go of anger, selfishness, and other negative behavior. They also do as much as possible to help the needy. Each day after the sun has set, fasting ends and

In larger cities, thousands of Muslims gather at a mosque for a daily prayer during Ramadan.

A town square comes alive with the dancing, drumming, singing, and colorful processions that are part of Eid-al-Fitr.

everyone enjoys a delicious meal. In the morning, the fast begins again.

When the next new moon comes, Ramadan is officially over. The following morning, to mark the end of fasting and this holiest of months, Muslims begin a three-day celebration known as Eid-al-Fitr. In Nigeria, Eid-al-Fitr is another national holiday.

On the first morning of Eid-al-Fitr, families get up early and dress in their best clothes. Teens and young children often receive new clothing and sometimes even get money or small gifts. If they have the means, families bring cash or dates, grains, or other foods to the mosque, where it will later be distributed to the poor. With everyone joined in this time of harmony and thankfulness, special prayers are offered. Soon afterward, it is time to begin celebrating.

In Nigeria's mostly Muslim northern states, the holiday celebration is especially vibrant and involved. In Katsina, the capital of Katsina state, thousands of Hausa and Fulani, dressed in their finest, flood into the arena in front of the palace of the emir, their religious leader.

While the excited crowd waits for the appearance of the emir, the activity in the arena intensifies. Jugglers, clowns, dancers, acrobats, and snake charmers move through the crowds. Hordes of men ride camels and horses draped in flashy silks.

Finally, the emir comes into view, at the head of a long, flamboyant procession. Dressed in orange and white robes, he is carried on a fancy chair shaded by a pink, embroidered umbrella. Marching on all sides of him

A rider and his horse wear bright, decorative costumes during the Durbar festival.

are bodyguards dressed in royal blue and deep red. Seeing their emir settle on the richly decorated stage before them, the crowd's excitement reaches its peak.

The highlight of Eid-al-Fitr is the Durbar, a spectacle of horsemanship. The ritual salutes the emir and signifies the highest respect. Once the Durbar is finished, the emir will address the crowd, then lead prayers at the mosque. Afterward Muslim families spend several days dancing, feasting, and visiting with friends before going back to the rhythms of their everyday lives.

The Masquerade

In southeastern Nigeria, a *mmanwu* festival—or masquerade—is a long-established and complex ritual. Several costumed figures in large, elaborately decorated masks dance to the beat of drums before an encircling crowd of villagers. These masked dancers, also called masquerades, perform a complex religious ritual dictated by ancient tribal custom.

Authentic masquerade dances have been slowly dying out. But all

mmanwu
mahn-WOO

Katsina Durbar

A breathless crowd waits in anticipation for the Durbar to get under way. They will know it has begun when they hear the pounding thunder of dozens of horse hooves. The crowd parts as several turbaned riders appear. Their horses, also draped in bright colors, gallop forward at full speed. Held high in their fists, razor-edged swords flash in the scorching sun. The men raise their voices in blood-curdling cries as they charge directly toward the emir. But no one moves to stop them.

At the last possible moment, only a few feet from their leader, the skilled horsemen rein in their mounts. The animals rise on their hind legs, and the charge is abruptly cut short. A billowing cloud of rust-colored dust envelops everything and then gradually thins out. Immediately, a second charge of riders rushes forward. Altogether, at least 20 groups of charging horsemen might participate in this dramatic ritual saluting the emir.

It is a spectacular sight that stirs the imagination, especially for young Muslim men. Many may dream of becoming horsemen in the Durbar themselves. Some will eventually succeed.

kinds of masquerades are still performed each year in ethnic communities throughout Nigeria, especially in Igboland. Whatever its form, the ritual is an important part of community life. Traditionally, its purpose is to enforce the community's moral codes of behavior.

The masquerade may portray a good or evil spirit, an ancestor, a villager who recently died, or one of the gods worshipped in the tribal religion. But exactly what the mask represents is known only to the masquerades.

The spirit supposedly makes its presence known in the form of the masquerade. Its purpose is to scold, to entertain, or to frighten someone who has done wrong or disobeyed the strict laws or customs of the community. Sometimes the masquerade's task is to release people from the clutches of what are believed to be evil spirits. The masquerade dance may also be performed to give thanks or ask for blessings from the gods or ancestors.

Mmanwu festivals often occur after the harvesting of crops or shortly before a new planting season begins. The most intense, private, and frightening masquerades are held in the dark of night.

Secret Societies

The masquerade is a ritual shrouded in secrecy. The identities of the masquerades are a heavily guarded secret, but they are always men. In some cases, women are forbidden to even look at the masks.

Masks are usually highly decorated and made of cloth, wood, and other natural elements. They are made in every size and shape. Some masks resemble faces. Others are shaped like helmets that cover the entire face. Still others are heavy, elaborate sculptures that tower in the air, displaying faces or human figures. Many masks have a soothing, beautiful quality and resemble women. Others have a fierce, masculine appearance and are purposely made to appear terrifying.

At a certain age, a young man may become a masquerade himself. But only those who are already part of this secret society will know about it. This knowledge, as well as what goes on during the initiation, are yet more deeply hidden secrets of the masquerade cults.

Hundreds of fishermen scour a river for fish during the Argungu fishing festival.

Many of the performers only appear at specific festivals or celebrations. Others may appear at several throughout the year. Today not all masquerades are private ceremonies for religious purposes. Masquerade festivals are also commonly held to entertain the public or tourists.

One Land, Many Festivals

Masquerades are not the only festivals enjoyed by the peoples of Nigeria's traditional religions. Many celebrations are not based on religion at all. In the waterways of the Niger Delta, regattas, or boat-racing festivals, are popular. Throughout many regions, the annual New Yam festival is a major event to celebrate the harvest of one of the nation's most important crops.

The Argungu Fishing Festival, which occurs toward the end of February in Argungu, Kebbi State, is another festival that hundreds of Nigerian teens look forward to each year. People from all over the world come to watch as men of all ages dive into the Argungu River for this lively competition. Whoever catches the biggest fish is the honored winner.

In a country rich in cultural diversity, Nigeria's teens get many opportunities to celebrate. No matter how different each of these occasions is or who attends them, a common thread ties them together. Virtually all celebrations in Nigeria reflect the people's vibrant energy and their love of song, dance, good food, and good times.

Since the demand for livestock in Nigeria's major cities is high, Nigerian teens often find jobs tending livestock.

5

Working Away

WITH RAZOR-SHARP MACHETES IN HAND, NIGERIAN TEENS FAN OUT ACROSS LARGE COCOA PLANTATIONS, READY TO JOIN THE HARVEST. Going from one tree to the next, they hack the large cacao seedpods from the trunks and limbs of the trees. Tucked inside these rough, yellowish pods is a precious product—dozens of wet cacao seeds, or cocoa beans. The beans are the main ingredient in one of the world's most popular treats: chocolate. They are also one of the most important agricultural crops in the nation. Nigeria is the fourth-largest exporter of cocoa beans in the world. This makes the cocoa belt, located within the country's tropical rain forest zone, an extremely valuable region.

Nigerian has three other distinct geographic regions as well. The northernmost zone lies just south of the Sahara Desert. It is made up of savannahs, or semiarid grasslands. Sparse patches of shrubs, tall grasses, and desert trees such as the locust bean and the baobab grow out of the sandy earth. This is the territory of the Hausa and the nomadic Fulani, who mainly raise large herds of cattle. Fulani teens are always on the move with their extended families as their clan searches for fresh grazing lands. Work is divided along traditional lines. The boys help care for the animals, and the girls are responsible, along with their mothers, for cooking, cleaning, and tending to children.

Large-scale farming, especially dairy and cattle farming, is another important form of work in this region. Besides beef and milk products, farms here produce some of Nigeria's most important crops, including cotton, sorghum, and groundnuts (peanuts).

Just south of the savannah, wide plateaus stretch to the horizon, where mountain ranges rise in irregular formations against the sky. This huge area is the heartland of the country. Rivers divide the land, and the climate is wetter and cooler than in the north. Here the land is rocky, so farms are generally smaller. Young people and their families raise sheep and goats. They grow crops such as maize, millet, plantains, cassava, yams, and potatoes. On most Nigerian farms, the work is time-consuming and tedious. Poverty-stricken village farmers cannot afford expensive, modern farm equipment. They cultivate the land using handmade plows and other simple tools.

Young people are also employed in the hard work of mining. This region is rich in mineral resources, such as iron ore, tin, coal, gold, limestone, and a black mineral called columbite.

The southernmost of the four geographical zones is the lowland coastal area. Midway along the coast, between stretches of white sandy beach and the countries of Cameroon on the east and Benin on the west, is the Niger Delta. Here, where the Niger River empties into the gulf, thick mangrove swamps grow in a tangle, and the land is laced

Teens cast large fishing nets into Nigeria's many rivers with the goal of catching fish for their families with enough left over to sell.

with a network of twisted waterways.

The delta region is also home to Nigeria's booming oil business. Oil is pumped from both land and sea, and petroleum products make up 95 percent of Nigeria's exports. Although some Nigerians may work in labor-intensive oil-industry jobs, such as drilling for the oil, few if any make it to the high-status power positions. These valuable resources are government-owned, but it is the big petroleum corporations that run the operation.

So while the

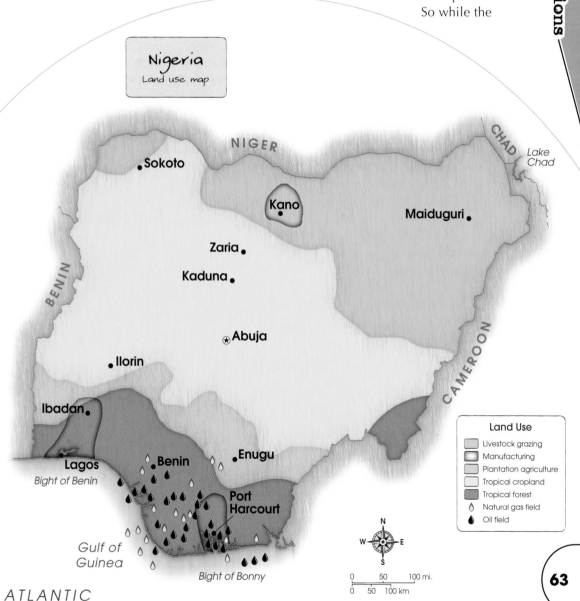

Nigeria
Land use map

NIGER

CHAD

Lake Chad

• Sokoto

Kano

Maiduguri •

BENIN

Zaria •

Kaduna •

⊛ Abuja

• Ilorin

Ibadan •

CAMEROON

Lagos
Bight of Benin

Benin

• Enugu

Port
Harcourt

Gulf of
Guinea

Bight of Bonny

Land Use

Livestock grazing
Manufacturing
Plantation agriculture
Tropical cropland
Tropical forest
Natural gas field
Oil field

N
W E
S

0   50   100 mi.
0   50   100 km

ATLANTIC
OCEAN

63

money may be pouring in to these corporations, the people of the Niger Delta remain impoverished.

Young people here are much more likely to be making their living in fishing-related industries. In fact, of the young people who work, more than 42 percent are employed in the areas of farming and fishing-related industries. Agriculture in the region is abundant. A few of the crops include rice, yams, cassava, rubber, and oil palm.

The rain forest zone, a wide, humid swath of territory, lies between the coastal zone and the plateau zone. Within it are three minizones. The heart of the rain forest is a place of towering, old-growth trees. A few of these tropical giants include mahogany, walnut, and iroko, also called African teak. In the forest industry, young men cut down trees or work in lumber mills. The rain forests also produce kola nuts, coffee, citrus trees, and countless other plants. But deforestation, the process of clearing forests for farming and timber, is taking a major toll on Nigeria's woodlands. Only 5 percent of the nation's rain forests remain.

The southeastern region of the rain forest is the palm belt. The tall oil palms that grow here produce a red fruit from which palm oil comes. Palm oil was once a major Nigerian industry because it goes into foods, moisturizers, soap, and many other products. But today, besides oil, gas, and cocoa beans, Nigeria's leading exports are rubber and cotton.

Cocoa beans may bring in less than 5 percent of Nigeria's money, but the work of harvesting them keeps some families alive. Once the cacao pods are hacked from the trees, they are split open with wooden clubs. Other young workers have the job of scooping

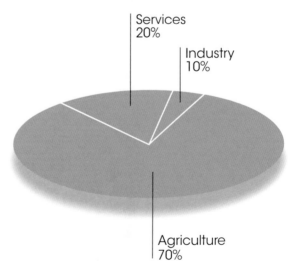

Division of Labor

Services 20%

Industry 10%

Agriculture 70%

Source: United States Central Intelligence Agency. *The World Factbook—Nigeria.*

the seeds out by hand. This is work that goes on year-round, but the main harvest season lasts from September through March.

Around the world, people will pay high prices for the best chocolate, but few of those harvesting the beans have ever tasted chocolate themselves. The working conditions can be brutal, and some of the laborers may even be young children. Some, in fact, may be slaves— children who have been kidnapped, sold by their parents, or unwittingly tricked into leaving home.

The existence of underage workers and child trafficking—the use of child labor for profit and the sale of children for work—occurs in industries throughout Nigeria, making it one of the nation's most severe and disturbing problems.

To Market

Only a few hours after sunrise, open-air markets are in full swing in Nigeria. Across a sprawling plot of land, owners of the many shacks and stalls enjoy brisk business as shoppers and sellers bargain and haggle. The atmosphere is noisy as dogs bark and children run and play games, squealing and laughing. The smells of grilled meat and ginger waft in the air. People crowd the stalls, many of them carrying their purchased goods on their heads.

Much of the produce grown throughout Nigeria eventually ends up in markets like this one. Virtually every village and small town has at least one

Child Work vs. Child Labor

According to Nigeria's Constitution, the country's youth deserve good schooling and a life that allows them to develop fully in all ways. The good intentions are there, but most young people are still missing out. Today many nongovernmental organizations (NGOs) are addressing the fate of overworked kids. They are looking for solutions.

These organizations make a distinction between child work and child labor. Child work is defined as work that does not prevent a young person from attending school. It does not expose a child to dangerous conditions or hazardous materials. Work includes the kind of everyday tasks, such as household chores, that are expected of any young person. It is limited to jobs that can be done in a reasonable amount of time and with breaks when working more than four hours. This kind of work can actually be helpful to a child's development. Just the opposite is true of child labor.

Street markets are constantly congested with hundreds of shoppers in large cities such as Lagos.

market where local produce is sold. The larger urban areas have several. Food of all kinds—fruits, vegetables, meats, spices, and roots—is for sale. So are local handicrafts, such as sculptures, carvings, beadwork, woven cloth, and batik, or tie-dyed fabrics.

Wherever there are markets, there are scores of teens. Many are selling their own wares. Others are planted in their parents' stalls. A teen who is not in school may spend the whole day working here. Those fortunate enough to be getting an education may still end up at the market after school, if trading provides some of the family's income. After school, young, hungry teens might grab a snack of *suya*, spicy-hot grilled meat, and then get on with their homework while sitting at their parents' stall. Many markets stay open until after dark, and only when they close down for the night does the family return home.

In southern Nigerian markets, women do most of the business of selling goods, while the men hold other jobs or professions. The market is an important part of life in the northern states as well. In the north, both rural and city markets are filled with young

suya
soo-YAH

children and teenage boys. But, because of purdah, few girls or women are ever seen there. Instead they work unseen. Like their mothers, teen girls are often industrious behind the scenes. They may cook bean cakes for sale, or a thick porridge called *tuwo*. Made from guinea corn, tuwo is a basic part of the Hausa diet. Some teens embroider or do other crafts. But whatever they intend to sell, in order to get their goods to

tuwo
too-WOH

Fast Food

Suya might be called a Nigerian form of fast food. Both teens and adults are in the business of selling it at markets and along the roadsides throughout the nation. The meat is usually beef but might also be chicken or goat meat. It is grilled, then sliced thin and slid onto skewers. It's served with a healthy sprinkling of hot red pepper and a heap of sliced red onions. The suya is so spicy that it causes tiny burns around the corners of a person's mouth—but that's the point. Karen Ekpenyong, a Nigerian who serves as dean of students at a school for girls in Chicago, Illinois, vividly recalls the experience of eating suya as a child. According to her, only a few bites and "you *have* to cry!" That's not only because of the spices, she explains, but also because "you just love it so much!"

market, women in purdah must rely on young children, who can come and go freely.

On the Streets

In Lagos, the capital of Lagos state and a teeming port city on the southeastern coast, the downtown streets become clogged with traffic in the afternoon. On every choked and dusty road, drivers are intent on making some progress without being hit. Although a temperature of 85 degrees Fahrenheit (29.4 degrees Celsius) is typical in Nigeria, it seems much hotter in the midst of this go-slow, or traffic jam.

The air is constantly filled with thick exhaust fumes and the angry blare of horns. Waves of heat rise from the metal roofs of the rickety and over-loaded old minibuses, called *danfos*, as they inch forward. Dozens of *okadas*, Lagos' lightweight motorbike taxis, buzz around

danfos
dahn-FOHS

okadas
oh-kah-DAHS

Commuters try to make their way through traffic on a crowded commercial road in Lagos.

and ahead of the bigger vehicles. Some of the okadas carry as many as four people. Everywhere, impatient, frustrated drivers endure the go-slow, hoping for some relief.

As the traffic crawls ahead, refreshments comes from scores of young street vendors, most of them teenage boys. Many girls and younger children also work the streets. They swarm around the vehicles like hoards of bees, hawking goods of all kinds. They sell plastic bags of cold water and fruit juice, peeled oranges, and kola nuts. The nuts, one of Nigeria's many agricultural crops, are used to make cola drinks. Loaded with caffeine, the nuts also give tired drivers a needed pick-me-up.

Besides food and drink, the young hawkers sell countless other goods. They offer flowers, newspapers, mousetraps, matches, sunglasses, and small packets of detergent and other household items. The money they make may be theirs to keep, or they may take it home to help their families buy a few of their own necessities.

Street vending is common throughout Nigeria, especially in other large cities, such as Kano in the north and the southwestern city of Ibadan, located north of Lagos in Oyo State. But young street vendors make up only a small portion of the 15 million Nigerians age 17 and under who work. City teens may find jobs in retail businesses, factories, or as head loaders—carrying heavy loads of merchandise from one place

Nigerian boys sell goods in the dangerous bumper-to-bumper traffic in Lagos.

to another on their heads. Many, including boys, work as domestic servants and housekeepers. Close to half of these young workers labor 15 hours a day or more, and only about 60 percent of them attend school.

Nigerian teens usually do not have the luxury of spending their money on things like dates or clothing. Instead, their earnings are often crucial to a family's survival. This is especially true in rural areas, where more than 70 percent of children begin working between the ages of 5 and 9. They are also more likely than their urban counterparts to work 15 hours a day.

Jobless and homeless, many Nigerian teens are forced to live on the streets.

Left Alone

The precise number of young people working the Nigerian streets is impossible to know. Some of them may be there out of choice. They may have homes to go to at the end of a long, hot day. But for hundreds of thousands of Nigerian youth, there is no home, no family. These are the neglected street kids living on their own in countless cities.

They sleep in abandoned buildings, in empty market stalls, and under bridges. They have no reliable source of food or clean water, and no one to protect them. They are teens, preteens, and even young children. Some have been abandoned by their adult caretakers. Others have run away from abusive households. Many are orphans, especially as a result of parental deaths from AIDS. In Nigeria, there are at least 1 million AIDS orphans.

According to recent studies, street children work even more hours than those with families. Those not attending school may work more than 16 hours a day. To survive, they try to find work. If not hawking goods, they take what work they can get. They might be hired to wash dishes in a *buka*, or restaurant. Some lay bricks, fetch water, or push broken vehicles to the side of the road for a few naira. More than a third of young street workers are load carriers.

buka
boo-KAH

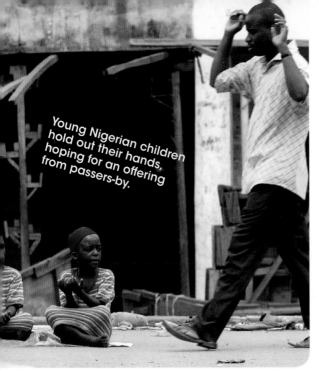

Young Nigerian children hold out their hands, hoping for an offering from passers-by.

Other teens beg or scavenge to stay alive, especially in the north. Scavengers dig through trash heaps hoping to find items they can sell. This kind of work is not just dirty. It's dangerous. The scavengers usually go barefoot and bare-handed. This can result in serious injuries and infections.

These are only a few of the dangers of life on the streets. Just as in rural areas, a young person alone is an easy target. Many become victims of criminal adults who make money through child trafficking. For too many Nigerian young people, life is more about work than anything else. And in many cases, it is certainly not work by choice.

Child Trafficking

International law prohibits this form of child labor, referring to it as a "practice similar to slavery." But that doesn't stop it from happening. Traffickers prey not only on young people, but also on financially troubled parents, who may be willing to sell their children.

Many teens and preteens are lured by the promise of high wages, education, or professional training. What they get instead is no pay and often brutal and abusive living conditions. Many are sold outright and shipped to other countries to work, and they have no way to get home. They are unlikely to ever see their families again. If they are not forced into prostitution—having to sell their bodies for money—most girls end up in market and domestic work. Boys are abandoned to various kinds of agricultural jobs.

Child trafficking is not just a problem in Nigeria. It occurs in numerous countries, making it a global tragedy. Estimates put the number of victims at more than 1 million worldwide.

Football, or soccer, is a popular pastime for many Nigerian teens.

6

Hang-Time, Nigerian Style

IN SIX OF NIGERIA'S MAJOR CITIES, THE HEAT IS ON. Thousands of young hopefuls gather in the nation's capital, Abuja, as well as in Lagos, Enugu, Benin, Ibadan, and Kaduna. They are there to audition for a television show in which solo contestants sing their hearts out before a panel of judges. Those who do well enough through many trials will end up in the finals and on TV. Each week, Nigerian viewers tune in to watch the performances and vote for the singer they like best. The five finalists will battle it out in song in hopes of becoming a national music icon.

The new show is from the Nigerian Television Authority (NTA), one of the nation's two government-run television networks. Called *Rising Star,* the interactive reality show grabs the attention of viewers across Nigeria.

However, the viewing audience is still not large since just under 25 percent of Nigerian homes have TVs.

Music Makers

Not every Nigerian teen wants to be a star, but music is at the heart of life throughout the nation. The country's rich musical heritage includes many forms, and its sounds are ever present in the air. Most of that music is driven by multiple, powerful rhythms that make it almost impossible to sit still when it's playing. Over the past 30 years, native musical styles such as juju music, Afrobeat, a combination of the two known as Afro-juju, and highlife have all been at the top of the charts.

These sounds are still popular, especially with older people. But Nigeria's teens have begun to go global in their musical tastes. Influenced especially by American and U.K. music and fashion, Nigeria's youth culture is exploding. Lagos, the nation's entertainment capital, is at the heart of that explosion. Lagos is home to scores of dance clubs, recording studios, film-production companies, and magazine publishers.

Rhythm and blues, pop, reggae, and jazz are all constants on radio and music-based TV channels. But some of the hottest music artists in Nigeria are those fusing traditional African sounds and styles with Western-style hip-hop—a trend often called Afro-pop. One Nigerian voice coming through more powerfully than most is that of 2Face Idibia. 2Face, one of the hottest young stars today, first got attention as part of Nigeria's highly successful R&B/hip-hop threesome, the Plantashun Boyz. When that group broke up in 2004, 2Face launched his solo career. After winning Best African Act at the 2005 MTV European Video Music Awards, he became an internationally

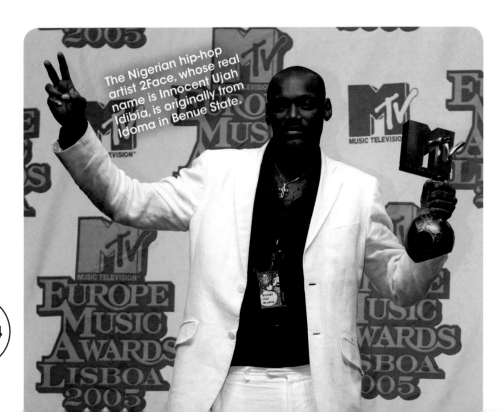

The Nigerian hip-hop artist 2Face, whose real name is Innocent Ujah Idibia, is originally from Idoma in Benue State.

Famous Nigerian Names

NIgeria has produced celebrities of all kinds, from musicians and athletes to a Nobel Prize-winning author.

King Sunny Ade

Probably the best known of all juju musicians is King Sunny Ade. Juju music is a Nigerian staple that originated with the Yoruba. In its updated form, it combines "talking drums," electric guitar, and a call-and-response vocal style, often with Yoruba lyrics.

Fela Kuti

Afro-beat, a style developed by Fela Kuti, is a combination of jazz and highlife. Kuti, who died in 1997, was both extremely popular and highly controversial. His songs dealt with things like the evils of dictatorships and what he believed was the viciousness of the Nigerian police force. His eldest son, Femi Kuti, followed in his father's musical footsteps. Femi continues to keep the Afro-beat sound alive today.

King Sunny Ade was nominated for a Grammy in 1998 with Odu, a collection of traditional Yoruba songs.

Hakeem Abdul Olajuwon

Nicknamed "Hakeem the Dream," Olajuwon was an outstanding basketball star in the 1980s. He played center with the Houston Rockets, part of the U.S. National Basketball Association.

Wole Soyinka

In 1986, Soyinka was the first Nigerian to win the highly respected Nobel Prize for Literature.

Although TV shows in Nigeria are full of entertainment, much of the airtime is used for government programs.

recognized star. Other young Nigerian celebrity singers include the group Styl-Plus, rapper Eldee, and female rapper Sasha.

Tube Time

If a Nigerian teen has the television on, there is a good chance he or she is watching Channel O or MTVbase, the African MTV channel. Highly popular with young people in Nigeria and elsewhere in Africa, both channels broadcast mostly music programming. The channels also have hip-looking Web sites with a lot of content. Besides TV, magazines like *Hip Hop World* and *Bubbles* keep young Nigerians informed about the world of music.

Music is not the only content available on Nigerian TV. One of the biggest broadcasters is Silverbird

Nigeria, a privately owned family entertainment network that reaches millions of viewers in Nigeria's southern states. Silverbird and other networks offer dramas, sitcoms, soap operas, sports, news, and talk shows. These include older American shows such as *Dharma and Greg*, *Ally McBeal*, *Martin*, and *Buffy, the Vampire Slayer*.

On Nigeria's government-owned stations, much of the programming is educational, but little of it is geared to young people. Regular broadcasts include shows that deal with child trafficking, prostitution, and other serious issues. A show on NTA called *Corruption Must Go* addresses the country's widespread problems with bribery, blackmail, and other forms of corruption. *Another Opportunity* is a reality show that gives former criminals a chance for a new, more productive life.

Teens who tune in to NTA can watch shows such as *Speak Out*, in which young Nigerians get the chance to voice their opinions on cultural, social, and political issues of the day. *I Need to Know* is a half-hour drama about young people dealing with issues of sex, HIV and AIDS, and relationships.

At the Movies

Trying to find a movie theater—someplace with a big screen and seats that lean back—is not easy in Nigeria. Real movie theaters are not widespread, even in major cities. Although it is growing rapidly, the movie industry is still just developing in Nigeria. Instead, people pick up videos from street hawkers or market stalls to view at home or even in restaurants.

Major Hollywood movies are always on the agenda, especially since Nigeria is an English-speaking country. But films from "Bollywood" and "Nollywood"— the nicknames for the film industries in India and Nigeria, respectively—are popular, too. Besides the English language, movie videos are available in the Hausa, Yoruba, and Igbo languages.

A National Passion

Football (soccer) games stir the energy and excitement of many Nigerian teens. In a typical village, up-to-the-minute hip-hop music plays on a portable radio as kids line up along the sides of a field, shouting and cheering. Others climb the mango trees that grow nearby or sit in the trees' leafy shade. A few wander among the crowd, offering groundnuts (peanuts) and yams for sale.

But most of the action takes place on the football field. The players do not wear helmets or thick padding. Instead most of them are dressed in casual shorts, and several are even barefoot. Even when it is being played on a rough patch of ground at the edge of town, football is the sport Nigerians are most passionate about. No matter how impoverished a village may be, the people love to play football. All it takes to get a game going are willing players and some kind of rubber ball.

In free moments, teenage boys may put together a casual game with

MTVbase

MTVbase launched in Africa in 2005 as MTV's 100th channel worldwide. It beams into 48 countries that lie south of the Sahara Desert, and at least 30 percent of its music content is from African artists. Other programs are twists on U.S. MTV shows, such as *Cribs*. On MTVbase, the hip houses that are featured belong to African soccer stars.

anyone who's up for joining in. But many belong to organized clubs that play other teams at the state or regional level. The national Nigerian Football Association's professional league includes 35 different football clubs. The NFA also sponsors many teams for teens. The Falconettes is the girls' under-19 team. The Golden Eaglets consists of youths from around the nation who are 17 or under. For countless Nigerian teens, the dream of a lifetime is to make it to the professional level. The best may one day play for Nigeria's national team, the Super Eagles.

Like young people everywhere in the world, Nigerian teens like dynamic physical activity of all kinds—not just football. Other popular sports, especially with boys, include basketball and boxing. Wrestling is another widespread activity among young men, especially the Igbo. Both boys and girls also play games such as table tennis and handball.

Children in the Nigerian village of Akaraolu play football during recess, while a gas flare burns brightly near them.

More Fun & Games

When they want to do something a little less physical, many young people play *ayo*. An ancient Yoruba game of skill, ayo is most often played on a carved wooden game board with seeds or beads used as game pieces. Two players compete to remove the opponent's pieces from pockets carved in the board until one player has all the beads.

In towns and villages known for their crafts, teens often learn these

pastimes from their elders. They may also spend time weaving, carving wood sculptures, or making jewelry.

Whether they live in big cities, small towns, or remote villages, Nigerian teens especially like to spend time just hanging out with friends. Malls are beginning to sprout up in some bigger cities, and young people gather in them to socialize. The cyberworld is also making inroads in Nigeria. On the streets of major cities, cyber cafés are

teens. If they are lucky, they might catch a glimpse of grazing elephants or even more rare forms of wildlife. The warm springs are in Yankari National Park, where hippos, lions, and antelope are only a few of the wild animals that roam free.

Because teens live in the area, they can take advantage of what the park has

A Life Without Luxuries

Most Nigerians do not own the kinds of conveniences that would make them part of the modern world. Besides the lack of televisions, cars, and landline phones, many homes are missing other things that most teens in the Western world take for granted:

- 65 of every 100 people own radios.
- 14 of every 100 homes have refrigerators.
- 7 of every 1,000 people own personal computers.
- 71 of every 1,000 people own cell phones.
- About 22 million of a population of more than 130 million have Internet access.

becoming more and more common. There teens who can afford it check their e-mail and connect with local friends and the rest of the world via the Internet. Although landlines may be scarce, wireless communication is becoming a booming business in Nigeria.

Beautiful Views

The lounge by the crystal-clear waters of the Wikki Warm Springs in Bauchi state is a popular hangout for groups of Nigerian

The clear water and relaxing atmosphere of Wikki Warm Springs draw tourists from countries around the world.

to offer. But until recently, tourism has not been highly promoted in Nigeria, especially with its own population. To many, this seems strange.

Nigeria is home to six national parks, as well as numerous game reserves, museums, and other excellent tourist attractions. It is the kind of place that adventurous tourists look for. There are dramatic differences in scenery, climate, and culture from one region to another. It has places of lush beauty, ancient ruins, and bustling, sophisticated cities. One can find the most modern scenes of everyday life as well as sights and sounds that seem straight out of biblical times. All this could make it a great place to visit.

Nigerians, however, rarely vacation as tourists within their own country. Teens and their families might travel across the entire country to visit friends. They will leave the city to spend their holidays hundreds of miles away in the villages they came from. But few can afford the luxury of travel just for sightseeing. Another reason Nigerians do not travel as tourists is that some parts of the country are unsafe, and traveling at night by car can be dangerous.

Because of extreme lawlessness in many parts of the country, travel in general is risky business. Not only criminals commit violent acts. News stories detail police and military atrocities against civilians, especially in the Niger Delta region, where ongoing conflict and kidnappings are related to the oil industry.

In the interest of safety, Nigerian families generally stick close to home. But that does not stop them from relaxing and enjoying time off. Nigerians are known to be especially warm, friendly, easygoing people. They know how to have a good time. All it takes is good company, good music, and maybe some great food.

National Park Treasures

Nigeria's national parks are rare treasures of wildlife and exotic plant species. Cross River National Park lies in southeastern Nigeria. This park is especially important to the nation because it is part of the last remaining rain forests. If the park is ever destroyed, Nigeria will forever lose many species of living things. The park is home to forest leopards, lowland gorillas, and the golden potto, a strange primate species.

Old Oyo National Park is in southwestern Nigeria. This park stretches across dense forestland and savannah where crocodiles, buffalo, and dozens of other animal species live. Also on this land are the ruins that gave the park its name. Before Fulani and Hausa armies destroyed it in the 18th century, Oyo was the capital city of a vast Yoruba empire.

Nigeria's largest (2,561 square miles; 6,659 square kilometers) and perhaps most scenic national park is Gashaka Gumti National Park in the northeast. GGNP, as it is often called, is home to many rare and endangered animal species. Some of the animals living here are cheetahs, colobus monkeys, and the giant forest hog. GGNP is also the site of Nigeria's highest mountain peak, the Chappal Waddi.

Every Nigerian national park and game reserve is important to the nation's ecological health. Poaching of animals and the destruction of forests for timber, wood products, and farmland are some of the country's most serious problems. These protected lands help the survival of animals, birds, and plant life that might otherwise be wiped out.

Looking Ahead

TEENS IN TODAY'S NIGERIA HAVE A DIFFICULT ROAD AHEAD OF THEM. In the nearly 50 years since becoming an independent nation, Naija has been continuously rocked by political change, and Nigeria's teens have felt the effects. For the youth of the nation, the future is at stake and the challenges are many. Simply finding common ground among various ethnic groups, religions, and traditions is a pressing challenge. Additionally, the country's teens must try to juggle a modern lifestyle with their traditional customs.

Educated, well-informed citizens are the main hope for Nigeria's survival as a unified nation. Those who complete their studies will achieve a global outlook and have opportunities that many of their parents never had. They will also have a huge impact on how their country develops. Their work is to correct the course that their country seems to be following. If they succeed, Nigeria could step out of chaos to become a stable, unified nation and a truly vibrant power on the world stage—led by those who today are only teenagers.

Is it possible? Given their heart and the passion they feel for their country, today's Nigerian youth may well grow into adults who can pull it off. Only time will tell.

At a Glance

Official name: Federal Republic of Nigeria

Capital: Abuja

People

Population: 131.9 million

Population by age group:
0-14 years: 42.3%
15-64 years: 54.6%
65 years and older: 3.1%

Life expectancy at birth: 47.1 years

Official language: English

Other common languages: Igbo, Yoruba, Fulani, Hausa, Edo, Efik, Adamawa Fulfulde, Idoma, Central Kanuri, and Yoniba

Religions:
Muslim: 50%
Christian: 40%
Indigenous beliefs: 10%

Legal ages
Alcohol consumption: No minimum
Driver's license: 18
Employment: No minimum
Leave school: After completing JSS
Marriage: No minimum
Military service: 18
Voting: 18

Government

Type of government: Federal republic with a presidential system

Chief of state: President

Head of government: President

Administrative divisions: Divided into the Federal Capital Territory (Abuja) and 36 states, organized into six zones

Independence: October 1, 1960 (from the United Kingdom)

National symbols: Green and white flag represents agriculture (green) and peace and unity (white); Nigerian coat of arms shows a black shield (representing Nigeria's fertile earth) flanked by two horses (dignity) and topped with a red eagle (strength). The shield has a Y shape in white, which represents the Niger and the Benue rivers.

Geography

Total area: 369,507 square miles (957,019 square kilometers)

Climate: Widely varying; equatorial in the south, arid in the north, tropical through the middle

Highest point: Chappal Waddi; 7,936 feet (2,420 meters)

Lowest point: Atlantic Ocean, sea level

Major rivers: Niger, Benue

Major landforms: Mandara Mountains, Chappal Waddi, Cameroon Highlands, Jos Plateau

Economy

Currency: Naira

Population below poverty line: 77%

Major natural resources: Petroleum, natural gas, limestone, tin, iron ore, coal, columbite, lead, zinc

Major agricultural products: Palm oil, millet, cassava, groundnuts, cacao, corn, rice, cotton, yams, beans, rubber, beef and hides

Major exports: Oil, cocoa, rubber

Major imports: Manufactured goods, machinery and transport equipment, chemicals, food, live animals

Historical Timeline

Britain begins to extend its control of Nigerian land, naming the region the Colony and Protectorate of Nigeria

Numerous city-states, empires, and kingdoms begin to develop across all parts of Nigeria, including the kingdoms of Ife, Hausa, Benin, and Kanem-Bornu

Slave trade booms until the 1860s; millions of Nigerians are enslaved and sent to the Americas

Yorubaland, in southern Nigeria, begins to experience constant civil war until 1886

| c. 500 B.C. | c. 1000 A.D. | 1472 | 1500s | 1809 | 1830s | 1851 | 1861 |

The British take control of Lagos

The Nok civilization is established across the Jos Plateau

The Sokoto caliphate, an Islamic state, is established in northern Nigeria; Islam spreads throughout the region, especially in the north

Portuguese sailors are the first Europeans to reach the Nigerian coast

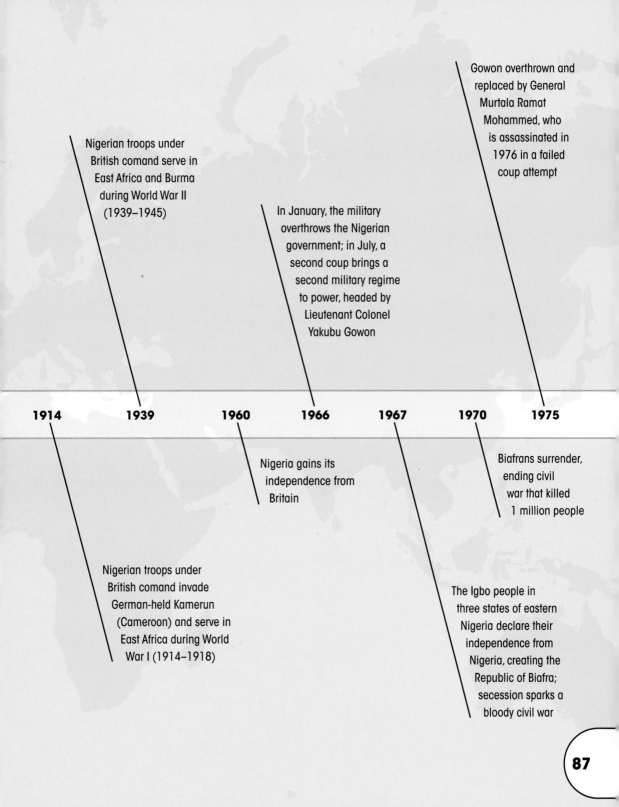

Nigerian troops under British comand serve in East Africa and Burma during World War II (1939–1945)

In January, the military overthrows the Nigerian government; in July, a second coup brings a second military regime to power, headed by Lieutenant Colonel Yakubu Gowon

Gowon overthrown and replaced by General Murtala Ramat Mohammed, who is assassinated in 1976 in a failed coup attempt

1914   **1939**   **1960**   **1966**   **1967**   **1970**   **1975**

Nigeria gains its independence from Britain

Biafrans surrender, ending civil war that killed 1 million people

Nigerian troops under British comand invade German-held Kamerun (Cameroon) and serve in East Africa during World War I (1914–1918)

The Igbo people in three states of eastern Nigeria declare their independence from Nigeria, creating the Republic of Biafra; secession sparks a bloody civil war

Historical Timeline

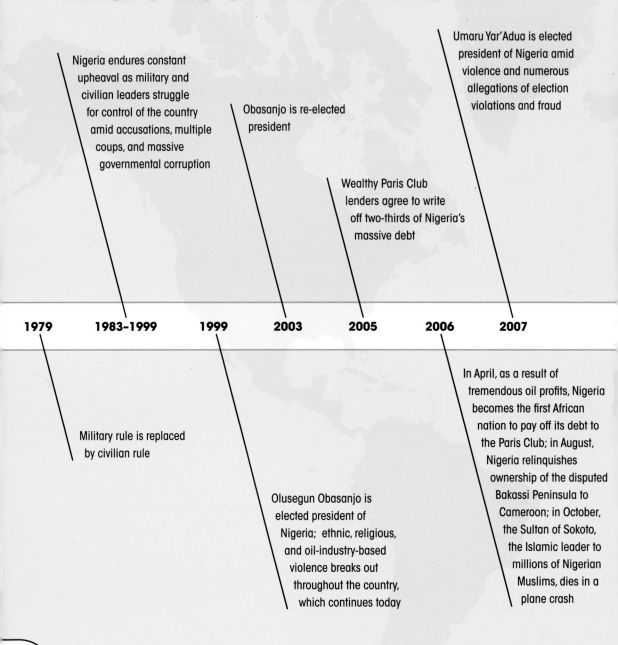

Nigeria endures constant upheaval as military and civilian leaders struggle for control of the country amid accusations, multiple coups, and massive governmental corruption

Obasanjo is re-elected president

Umaru Yar'Adua is elected president of Nigeria amid violence and numerous allegations of election violations and fraud

Wealthy Paris Club lenders agree to write off two-thirds of Nigeria's massive debt

1979   **1983–1999**   **1999**   **2003**   **2005**   **2006**   **2007**

Military rule is replaced by civilian rule

Olusegun Obasanjo is elected president of Nigeria; ethnic, religious, and oil-industry-based violence breaks out throughout the country, which continues today

In April, as a result of tremendous oil profits, Nigeria becomes the first African nation to pay off its debt to the Paris Club; in August, Nigeria relinquishes ownership of the disputed Bakassi Peninsula to Cameroon; in October, the Sultan of Sokoto, the Islamic leader to millions of Nigerian Muslims, dies in a plane crash

Glossary

AIDS	abbreviation for Acquired Immune Deficiency Syndrome, a disease of the immune system that makes people more likely to catch infections and some rare cancers that are often fatal; usually transmitted by sexual activity
apprenticeships	periods of time spent training in a particular field with an expert or professional in that field
curriculum	the courses of study offered at an educational institution
emir	religious leader in Islamic countries
indigenous	native to a place
mallam	Muslim scholar
mosque	the Islamic place of worship
nomadic	relating to roaming around from place to place
polygyny	having multiple wives; a form of polygamy
prevocational	education or training that occurs before vocational school
Qur'an	the holy book of Islam, which consists mainly of the revelations Muhammad received from God during the 17th century
secular	having to do with non-religious matters

Additional Resources

IN THE LIBRARY

Fiction and nonfiction titles to further enhance your introduction to teens in Nigeria, past and present.

McCall Smith, Alexander. *Akimbo and the Elephants*. New York: Bloomsbury's Children's Books, 2005.

Naidoo, Beverley. *The Other Side of Truth*. New York: HarperCollins, 2001.

Stolz, Joelle. *The Shadows of Ghadames*. New York: Delacorte Press, 2004.

Williams-Garcia, Rita. *No Laughter Here*. New York: HarperCollins, 2004.

Hamilton, Janice. *Nigeria in Pictures*. Minneapolis: Lerner Publications, 2003.

Nnoromele, Salome. *Nigeria*. San Diego: Lucent Books, 2002.

Rosenberg, Anne. *Nigeria: The Culture*. New York: Crabtree Publishing Company, 2001.

ON THE WEB

For more information on this topic, use FactHound.
1. Go to www.facthound.com
2. Type in this book ID: 0756533066
3. Click on the Fetch It button.

Look for more Global Connections books.

Teens in Australia
Teens in Brazil
Teens in Canada
Teens in China
Teens in Egypt
Teens in England
Teens in France

Teens in India
Teens in Iran
Teens in Israel
Teens in Japan
Teens in Kenya
Teens in Mexico
Teens in Russia

Teens in Saudi Arabia
Teens in South Korea
Teens in Spain
Teens in Venezuela
Teens in Vietnam

Source Notes

Page 12, sidebar, column 1, line 21: "Sustainable Africa." *AllAfrica.com*. 14 March 2007. http://allafrica.com/sustainable/

Page 12, sidebar, column 2, line 11: "The Nigerian Constitution." *The Federal Republic of Nigeria*. 2 April 2007. www.nigeriahcottawa.com/eduinfo/constitution_cht2.htm

Page 12, sidebar, column 2, line 19: "Sustainable Africa." *AllAfrica.com*. 14 March 2007. http://allafrica.com/sustainable/

Page 25, column 2, line 7: Ogbu Kalu. Personal interview. 23 Jan. 2007.

Page 29, column 1, line 10: Paul Kalu. Personal interview. 4 Feb. 2007.

Page 46, column 2, line 3: Randy Fogg. "Nigeria Project." 5 April 2001. http://nigeriaproject.emporia.edu/andover401.htm

Page 42, sidebar, line 8: Nkoli Ezumah. "Perception of Womanhood in Nigeria and the Challenge of Development." 11 March 2007. http://www.gwsafrica.org/knowledge/nkoli.htm

Page 67, sidebar, line 19: Karen Ekpenyong. Personal interview. 17 Feb. 2007.

Page 71, sidebar, column 1, line 3: "Child Labor." *Human Rights Watch*. 8 Jan. 2007. www.hrw.org/children/labor.htm

Pages 84–85, At a Glance: United States. Central Intelligence Agency. *The World Factbook—Nigeria*. 17 April 2007. 30 April 2007. www.cia.gov/library/publications/the-world-factbook/geos/ni.html

Select Bibliography

"Child Labor." *Human Rights Watch.* 8 Jan. 2007. www.hrw.org/children/labor.htm

Clark, Nick, and Robert Sedgwick. "Education in Nigeria." *World Education News & Reviews* 17.5 (2004). 17 March 2007. www.wes.org/ewenr/04Sept/Practical.htm

"A Country Profile: Nigeria." *Library of Congress Federal Research Division.* June 2006. 2 Feb. 2007. http://memory.loc.gov/frd/cs/ngtoc.html

Dayrell, Elphinstone. "Folk Stories From Southern Nigeria." 2 March 2007. www.sacred-texts.com/afr/fssn

Ekpenyong, Karen. Personal Interview. 17 Feb. 2007.

Ezumah, Nkoli. "Perception of Womanhood in Nigeria and the Challenge of Development." 11 March 2007. http://www.gwsafrica.org/knowledge/nkoli.htm

Falola, Toyin. *Culture and Customs of Nigeria.* Westport, Conn.: Greenwood Press, 2001.

Falola, Toyin. *Teen Life in Africa.* Westport, Conn.: Greenwood Press, 2004.

"Fela Kuti." *Fela Kuti Project.* 5 March 2007. www.felaproject.net

Fogg, Randy. "Nigeria Project." 5 April 2001. http://nigeriaproject.emporia.edu/andover401.htm

Global Youth Coalition on AIDS/HIV. *GYCA.* 23 Feb. 2007. www.youthaidscoalition.org

Kalu, Ogbu. Personal Interview. 23 Jan. 2007.

Kalu, Paul. Personal Interview. 4 Feb. 2007.

"Nigeria." *Embassy of the Federal Republic of Nigeria, Washington, D.C.* 12 Feb. 2007. www.nigeriaembassyusa.org/students.shtml

"Nigeria." *Rainforestweb.org.* 23 Feb. 2007. www.rainforestweb.org/Rainforest_Regions/Africa/Nigeria/

"Nigeria May Be Left Without Forest by 2010." *Terra Daily.* 18 Jan. 2007. 25 Feb. 2007. www.terradaily.com/reports/Nigeria_May_Be_Left_Without_Forest_By_2010_999.html

"The Nigerian Constitution." *The Federal Republic of Nigeria*. 2 April 2007. www.nigeriahcottawa.com/eduinfo/constitution_cht2.htm

"Nigeria's Information Portal." *Online Nigeria*. 22 Jan. 2007. www.onlinenigeria.com

O'Connell, Meaghan. "Ayo: The Yoruba Game Board." 28 Jan. 2007. www.african-museum.com/discover/1meaghan/ayo.htm

"The Official Information Gateway of the Federal Republic of Nigeria." *Nigeria Direct*. 21 March 2007. www.nigeria.gov.ng/

"Population of Nigeria." *Population World*. 9 May 2007. www.populationworld.com/Nigeria.php

"Sexual Cultures." *Feminist Africa 5* (2005). 12 Dec. 2006. www.feministafrica.org/2level.html

"Sports." *The Nigerian Embassy*. 17 March 2007. www.nigerianembassy-chile.org/nigeria/xsports.shtml

"Summary Education Profile: Nigeria." *Worldbank*. 17 March 2007. http://devdata.worldbank.org/edstats/SummaryEducationProfiles/CountryData/GetShowData.asp?sCtry=NGA,NIGERIA

"Sustainable Africa." *AllAfrica.com*. 14 March 2007. http://allafrica.com/sustainable/

U.S. Department of Labor. Bureau of International Labor Affairs. *Advancing the Campaign Against Child Labor, vol. III: The Resource Allocations of National Governments and International Financial Institutions*. 29 Jan. 2007. www.usembassy.it/pdf/other/advance.pdf

United States. Central Intelligence Agency. *The World Factbook—Nigeria*. 17 April 2007. 30 April 2007. www.cia.gov/library/publications/the-world-factbook/geos/ni.html

"World Telecommunication Development Report." *International Telecommunication Union*. 2004. 8 Jan. 2007. www.itu.int/net/home/index/aspx

Index